A CONVERSATION BOOK 1
English in Everyday Life
Revised Third Edition
TEACHER'S GUIDE

Tina Kasloff Carver

Sandra Douglas Fotinos

Prentice Hall Regents

D1206190

Publisher: Louisa B. Hellegers

Development Editor: Barbara Barysh
Electronic Production Editor: Steven D. Greydanus
Art Director: Merle Krumper
Manufacturing Manager: Ray Keating
Illustrator: Andrew Lange

Our thanks to Nancy Baxer and
Ki Chul Kang who were the
motivating forces behind this
third edition.

PRENTICE HALL REGENTS

Printed in the United States of America
10 9 8 7 6 5

0-13-792441-0

CONTENTS

UNIT 1: WELCOME TO CLASS   1

UNIT 2: EVERYDAY LIFE

UNIT 3: THE CALENDAR 25

UNIT 4: FOOD

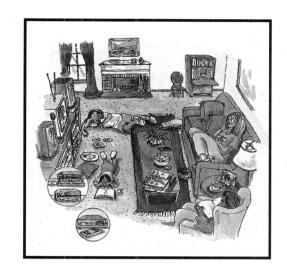

UNIT 5: HOMES

UNIT 6: SHOPPING 81

UNIT 7: COMMUNITY 105

UNIT 8: WORK

UNIT 9: HEALTH   149

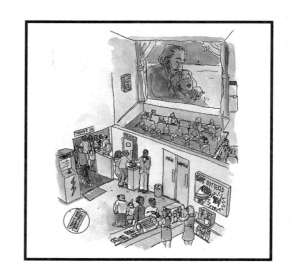

UNIT 10: LEISURE

APPENDIX

Tests

A Writing Book Correlations

TO THE TEACHER

We have written this **Teacher's Guide** to serve as a springboard for your own creativity and individuality in the classroom. New teachers may want to use our suggestions as a guide; experienced teachers may want to use the book as a resource for an occasional explanation of an unfamiliar activity or to find alternative ideas for warm ups, activities in the class, and expansion activities. Remember what works in one class may not work in another. Mark the pages in the **Teacher's Guide**, noting what works and what doesn't work in your classes. You may want to note HOW the activity worked better for you with your own twist to it. It is in this spirit that we offer this book to you. It is not meant to be used as a bible or a cookbook. Try not to follow the directions to the "letter of the law," but to make it your own resource guide.

A few of the procedures are formulaic. In the interest of saving space and avoiding repetition in the body of the **Teacher's Guide**, we have provided the basic procedures for introducing vocabulary and working through the activities with the students.

NOTEBOOKS

It would be useful for the students to have a notebook and divide it into four sections: **Vocabulary**, **Community Information**, **Activities**, and **Journal**. Students should use the **Vocabulary** section to write new words not in the text. The **Community Information** section should be for pertinent information about their communities. The **Activities** section should be used to do the various activities and assignments in the text as well as **Expansion Activities** from the **Teacher's Guide**. The **Journal** section can be used for additional journal writing after the students have been introduced to writing journals.

LEARNING STRATEGIES

The Learning Strategies box on the first page of every unit suggests ways to facilitate learning for the unit. The objective of these strategies is to guide students to be independent learners. Discuss each strategy with the students as you begin the unit. Have students concentrate on the strategies throughout the unit and have them continue to practice the strategies from previous units. Add strategies as everyone in the class becomes aware of his or her unique learning style. Review them all at the end of each unit.

Read out loud the introduction (To the Student) from Professor H. Douglas Brown and discuss the advantages of understanding how each individual has his or her own way to learn most effectively.

ORGANIZATION OF THE LESSONS

Warm Up

Every lesson has a warm up activity. We have tried to vary these as much as possible. Some use picture files or photos, some use realia, some have students brainstorming lists of words. The warm up activities all prepare the students to begin to think about the topic of the lesson.

Students can prepare their notebooks either before or after the warm up by opening to a page in the **Vocabulary** section and writing the name of the lesson at the top of the page. Then they can note new words on this page and if they wish, write their native language equivalent next to the word. This becomes their personalized list of English vocabulary. Encourage students to form the habit of copying the important words, phrases, and information into their notebooks. You might need to remind them at the beginning of the class that they should be transferring the notes from the board to their notebooks.

In the Text

Vocabulary

- Look at the illustration with the students or show the transparency with the books closed. (Having the books closed and the students looking at the transparency focuses the students on the lesson and on you, not words on a page.)
- If you don't have the transparencies, have students cover the words with a card or with their hands.
- Model each vocabulary word. If you prefer, use the audiotaped vocabulary lists to model the words.
- Give students the opportunity to repeat as you model the pronunciation. Listen for pronunciation and correct as necessary.
- Point to the corresponding illustration as you say the word.
- *Variation:* As you point to an illustration, have students tell you the number of the word from the vocabulary box. You can vary this later; give a number and have students come to the transparency, point out the corresponding illustration and pronounce the word.
- Write the number of each word on the corresponding illustration either in your book or on the transparency with an erasable marker. (Place a blank transparency over the illustration transparency; mark and write on the blank one. This will preserve your illustrated transparencies.) Have students mark the numbers on the illustrations in their texts.
- Be sure students understand the words. Discuss meanings and uses of the words.
- Ask students if they can tell you any words they know that are NOT on the list and that are relevant to the topic. Write those words on the board. Ask if students remember seeing any of the words in an earlier unit. Have them check the Vocabulary Word List in the back of their texts to be sure. Remember that words appear in the vocabulary boxes only once, although subsequently, the word may be illustrated.
- Have students copy the new student-generated words on the board into their texts in the blanks provided. Have them number this vocabulary.

Activities

Each lesson has several activities. The section **Suggestions for Teaching Activities** provides step-by-step instructions for possible ways to teach each of the different kinds of activities in the lessons. There are also detailed instructions for each new activity on the corresponding Teacher's Guide page, as well as page references back to the lesson in which any repeated activity was first presented.

Expansion Activities

Expansion activities can be found at the end of each lesson. The wide variety of activities gives you and the students the opportunity to close the texts and work with the vocabulary and topics relevant and useful outside the structure of the text.

REVIEW

At the end of each unit is a Review page with activities to review the whole unit.

TESTS

Conversation Tests and Vocabulary Tests for all units are located in the back of the Teacher's Guide. Feel free to make as many copies as you need.

CONVERSATION SPRINGBOARDS

Here are dialogs for teachers who hate dialogs! We have developed these springboards as conversation starters, to serve as models and inspirations for students to talk about their life experiences. They are not designed to be used for pattern practice! They are intentionally longer than traditional dialogs because they are meant for listening to and understanding real, whole conversations about everyday life in English. An accompanying Audio Program is available, which includes all of these Conversation Springboards.

Cassette icons [icon] on student-text pages signal where to use the audiotape for discrete vocabulary practice as well as for a cross-reference to the Appendix page with the corresponding Conversation Springboard.

There are five types of Conversation Springboards: *What's the process?*, *What's happening?*, *What happened?*, *What's next?*, and *What's your opinion?* Each type has a specific purpose.

- *What's the process?* Conversation Springboards are to be used *before* specified activities, and are intended to help students understand and talk about the purpose and process of the activity, as well as possible complications and their solutions.
- *What's happening?* Conversation Springboards tell a story, happening in the present. These dialogs are intended to help students listen to conversational narratives in present time, and to retell stories chronologically, using present and present progressive tenses.
- *What happened?* Conversation Springboards relate a story that happened in the past, and give students practice listening to past-time narratives and retelling the events in order, using past tenses.
- *What's next?* Conversation Springboards tell a story without an ending, or with a next step implied but not stated. They give students practice in drawing conclusions from indirect information, as well as opportunities to create their own endings in future time.
- *What's your opinion?* Conversation Springboards present a situation where preferences and opinions are expressed, and give students opportunities to agree or disagree with them, express their own opinions, and participate in a class discussion of a topic.

We suggest the following method of using the Conversation Springboards and accompanying Audio Program:

1. Listen to the entire conversation once, with books either open or closed, depending on the class level and preference.

2. Listen again, breaking up the conversation by stopping the tape after every two lines. Check for understanding. Define any words that are unclear. Whenever possible, have students write down words they're not sure of and try to guess the meaning from context.

3. Listen to the entire dialog again. (If you have listened with books closed until now, listen with books open this time.)

4. Follow up by having students either explain the process, situation, or problem, or tell the story of the conversation, depending on which type of Conversation Springboard you are using.

5. You may wish to have students read the conversations out loud themselves, depending on the class level and preference. If you do, go slowly! Remember that these are beginning students and long conversations!

GRAMMAR FOR CONVERSATION

The Grammar for Conversation section of the Appendix consists of conversation–based grammar charts and lists for each unit. The charts focus on basic grammar constructions and lists of formulaic expressions that students need to use extensively in each unit. The grammar emerges from the conversations and activities in the unit and the Conversation Springboards.

The conversations in this book are not grammar based. On the contrary, the practical needs of conversation in everyday life form the basis of the grammar included in the text. As a result, many grammar constructions appear very early in the book. They are intended to serve as springboards for understanding and using grammar in the context of everyday conversation, not for studying the grammar of English in a more conventional, systematic way. Each grammar element in a chart or list appears only once in the Appendix, although the same grammar element can occur throughout the book. Thus, students should be encouraged to refer to grammar charts from early units continually throughout the semester. You might want to teach and/or review a particular construction for an activity before or after the activity. However, the emphasis should be on conversation and communication, not grammatical accuracy.

In keeping with the **CONVERSATION BOOK** philosophy, the Conversation Springboards and Grammar for Conversation serve as beginnings—ways to get started listening and talking with the class, and ways to spark individual thinking and creativity. English may be a new language to your students, but that newness should not prevent them from using it creatively and having fun in the process of learning it. Most of all, have fun with these conversations!

CORRECTIONS

Use your own best judgment in handling corrections. Too much correction inhibits students' ability to think coherently and works contrary to practicing coherent and fluent conversation skills. On the other hand, aim to strike a balance, teaching syntax as well as pronunciation at opportune times. Take note of the errors students are making. It is usually not helpful to interrupt the flow of students' conversations, but correct errors at the appropriate time later in class, without referring to any specific students.

GROUPING

Pairing partners can be done in a variety of ways. The easiest way is to have students seated next to each other be partners. However, since an objective of the partner activities is for students to get to know one another, having a variety of partners is essential. Pairing students in different ways maintains students' attention, moves them around the room, and helps them to learn each other's names.

Suggestion:
- Count the students in the class; then divide them in half by left side/right side or front/back.
- Hand out slips of paper to one half of the students.
- Ask them to write their full names on the paper and fold the paper.
- Collect all the folded papers, then walk through the other half of the class. Have each student pick one folded paper.
- When all the papers are handed out, instruct the students with the papers to find their partners and sit down together.
- Depending on the class (and your own teaching style), you may prefer an open free-for-all with everyone walking around at once, calling out names; or a more structured pairing may be more appropriate in which one student at a time reads the name on his or her paper. The student named raises his or her hand, and the two then sit together.

These methods of pairing can be used again and again, dividing the class in different ways to assure that students have many different partners and get to know everyone in the class by name.

Partners should always ask each other for their names; there is a place in each **Partner Activity** for students to write their **Partner's Name**.

For some activities, *larger groups* of students are necessary. Again, grouping students can be done in a variety of ways.

Suggestion:
- Have students count off numbers (1–4, 1–5, 1–6, etc.), then join those who have that number.
- To practice vocabulary, you may replace numbers with items from the current vocabulary list—colors, fruits, vegetables, flowers, seasons, etc.
- List the group names on the board (for example, with colors, Red, Black, Yellow, Green, etc.), then assign each student a color and have students form groups according to their assigned color.

After students get to know each other, informal methods of pairing or grouping usually work best. Sometimes you can let students choose a partner or set up their own groups. For other activities, depending on the subject matter, you may want to deliberately mix gender, ages, language groups, occupations, or opinions. Try to avoid cliques sitting together. Remind students that the only way to develop conversational fluency in English is to practice *in English*.

TRANSPARENCIES

A boxed set of **Color Transparencies** is available. These transparencies include ALL the illustrations from the picture dictionary pages of the full edition. The transparencies can facilitate the introduction of the vocabulary lesson by allowing students to close their books and look up, rather than being engrossed in words and page turning. The transparencies focus students' attention and enable teachers to point out details more easily. The transparencies can also be used for class activities, for vocabulary review and as an alternative testing instrument.

SUGGESTIONS FOR TEACHING ACTIVITIES

Class Activities

1. Community Activity
OBJECTIVE: To get to know the community and its resources.

There are a variety of activities either using community resources (i.e., the telephone book) or the community at large (i.e., the supermarket). The instructions vary from activity to activity, but the objective is always to get students to become familiar with their community, to become aware of English, and to practice English within the context of everyday surroundings.

- Review the task before students are asked to do the work independently. Be sure students know the vocabulary and are clear about what they are to do.
- Help prepare students; role-play expected scenarios and outcomes. This may avoid pitfalls and panic!
- If possible, accompany the class the first time out. This will give them confidence.
- After the students do the assignment, review it in class.
- Discuss not only the task but what happened—what surprises they had, what reactions they had, how they felt, etc.
- Have students record important community information in the **Community** section of their notebooks.

2. Cross-Cultural Exchange
OBJECTIVE: To exchange information about students' cultures.

- Ask the questions and have students explain their customs.
- Find out how many different languages and cultures students know about. Be sure the discussion includes everyone's culture!
- Whenever possible, have students teach the class how to say something in their native language or tell the class something interesting about their culture, or a culture that may not be theirs, but they know about.

3. Discussion
OBJECTIVE: To integrate new vocabulary into the context of students' experiences; to listen to other students' experiences and take notes.

- Ask the questions and call on different students for the answers.
- Involve as many students as possible in the discussion.
- Write new vocabulary on the board as it comes up in conversation.
- Use the information students offer to draw conclusions and teach students about different ways of life.
- Help structure discussions and teach note-taking skills. Write a brief heading for each question on the board. Encourage students to do the same in the **Activities** section of their notebooks.
- List information you gather from the discussions under each heading.
- Review your notes and ask the students to review theirs. Draw conclusions together from the notes at the end of the discussions.

4. Find Someone Who

OBJECTIVE: To practice asking yes/no questions; to share personal information with classmates.

- Review the vocabulary.
- Write the first question on the board.
- Ask the question to individual students until you get a "yes" answer. Then write the response on the board, using the student's name.
- Repeat this procedure for the other questions. Be sure students understand all the vocabulary.
- Review grammatical structures.
- Have students circulate and ask each question. If the class is very large, divide it into groups of 10-15 and have students do the activity within their groups.
- When students find a "yes" answer, instruct them to write that student's name in the correct space.
- *Variation:* instruct them to ask that student to sign his or her name in the correct space.
- As students complete the activity, have them sit in their seats.
- Call on individual students to give the answers to each question.
- Take advantage of interesting information about the class generated by this activity.

5. Games

TPR

OBJECTIVE: To associate words with actions; to reinforce learning; to practice responding to and giving commands.

- In preparation, give out slips of paper to each student.
- Model all actions with exaggerated movements.
  Think: Show yourself thinking.
  Write: Write an appropriate word or command. Use a dark marking pen on a piece of paper. Hold it up for the class to see. Have students write their own responses on their slips of paper.
  Fold: Fold your paper. Have students fold their papers.
  Make a pile: Put your folded paper on your desk. Have students come up and put their folded papers on top of yours. The papers should form a pile. Shuffle the pile.
  Open one: Open the first one. Read it.
  Guess: Model guessing or ask, "What am I doing?" and do the action (depending upon the activity).
- Whoever guesses correctly gets to pick the next slip.
- Continue as long as interest and/or time allow.

Vocabulary Challenge

OBJECTIVE: To review vocabulary; to sharpen memory recall skill.

- Show students the transparency for the lesson or direct their attention to the illustration in the text.
- Have students use a page in the **Vocabulary** section of their notebooks and write all the vocabulary they can remember, either using the illustration as a prompt or using their memories. They should not look at the words.
- Tell students to number their words so they can count how many they remembered.
- Give a five minute time frame. Then have individual students tell the class how many words they remembered.
- Have several students read their lists to the class or write the lists on the board.
- Instruct students to copy the new words into the **Vocabulary** section of their notebooks.

6. Strip Story
OBJECTIVE: To state problems; to find solutions; to tell stories.

- Look at each frame of the story separately. Use the open text or the transparency.
- Ask what is happening. Have students state the problem first and then tell you what is happening and what the outcome is.
- Decide with the class what to write as a caption for each frame. Supply vocabulary as needed.
- Have the students copy the captions into their texts or into the **Activities** section of their notebooks.

Group Activities

1. Conversation Squares
OBJECTIVE: To interview students and classify information.

- Have the students help you create the questions they will need for each square.
- Write the questions on the board.
- Construct boxes on the board similar to the ones in the text.
- Choose two students. Use yourself as the third member of the group.
- Put the three names on the top of the boxes as indicated in the text.
- Ask and answer the questions for your box; write in your responses.
- Ask your "partners" the questions. Write their responses.
- Then ask the class the questions for more practice.
- Have groups of three do the activity.
- When all groups have finished, ask different groups single questions from the conversation squares. Put new vocabulary on the board for students to write in the **Vocabulary** section of their notebooks.

2. Decision
OBJECTIVE: To practice discussing issues and coming to consensus.

- Divide students into the suggested groupings.
- Read the instructions together. Be sure everyone understands the task.
- Have each group select a *leader* to ask the questions or pose the problem, a *recorder* to write down the group's decisions, and a *reporter* to tell the class what the group's decision was.
- When the groups have finished their task, have all reporters give short summaries of the decisions.
- Take advantage of interesting outcomes—similar opinions, differences, other facts. What happens if a group can't agree? Talk about that too!

3. Discussion
OBJECTIVE: To listen to questions and respond within a group setting.

This is similar to the Discussion in Class Activities, but students are in small groups instead.
- Divide the class into the suggested groupings.
- Have each group select a *leader* to ask the questions and a *recorder* to take notes.
- When all groups have completed the activity, have the recorder report back to the class.
- *Variation:* also have each group select a *reporter* to tell the class what the group decided.
- Use interesting information from the discussion as a springboard for further conversations.

4. Games

Gossip!
OBJECTIVE: To listen to and repeat a story with details.

- Have students close their books.
- Divide the class into groups of eight.

- Have each group choose a *leader*.
- Explain words "whisper" and "secret."
- Have all leaders open their **student texts** to the **Gossip Secrets** in the **APPENDIX**, and silently read the secret several times. All other students should have their books closed.
- Ask the leaders from each group to close their books and whisper the secret to the student sitting next to them.
- Have that student whisper the secret to the next student.
- This should continue until all the students have heard the secret.
- Have the last student in each group come to the board and write the secret on the board.
- Then read the secret aloud to the whole class.
- Ask: What information was omitted? What was changed? Which group had the best information?

Pantomime
OBJECTIVE: To associate actions with words and understanding; to practice gestures.

- Do a few practice pantomimes with the whole class.
- Divide the class into the suggested groupings.
- Have students take turns doing the pantomimes. Have others in the group guess what that student is doing.
- Have the student who guesses do the next pantomime, or have students take turns around the circle.
- Review the activity with the whole class. Have one person from each group do a pantomime and have the class guess.

Vocabulary Challenge
OBJECTIVE: To review the vocabulary of the lesson; to add new words to the students' vocabulary.

- Divide the class into the suggested groupings. Have each group select a *recorder*.
- Allow students to look at the transparency for the lesson.
- Instruct students to make one list per group.
- Give students a specific time limit for completing the list.
- Tell the recorders to write the list of words and expressions as students dictate them. Remind the recorder to number their words so they can count how many they remembered.
- When time is up, have each group's recorder read their list to the class or have the recorders write their lists on the board.
- Compare lists. Which group had the longest list? the most new words?
- Have students copy the new words into the **Vocabulary** section of their notebooks.

What is it?
OBJECTIVE: To integrate vocabulary; to ask yes/no questions about the classroom through an information gap activity.

- Read the instructions aloud with the students.
- Demonstrate possible yes/no questions.
- Write these questions on the board.
- Have students suggest other yes/no questions.
- Divide the class into the suggested groupings.
- To demonstrate, be the *leader* first in one group. Have the other groups observe.
- Make a statement. Have students ask you yes/no questions. When a student guesses what you are thinking of, that student becomes the leader and the game continues. You are now part of the group to ask and guess.
- Review any new vocabulary and write it on the board.
- Have students copy the new words into the **Vocabulary** section of their notebooks.

5. Problem Posing/Problem Solving
OBJECTIVE: To come to group consensus about stating a problem; to arrive at a group solution.

- Divide the class into the suggested groupings.
- Have each group pick a *reporter*.
- Instruct the groups to decide what the problem is.
- Have the groups make one statement of advice, suggesting a solution for the problem.
- Have each reporter state the problem and the solution to the class.
- Compare solutions. Have the class decide which solution was best for each problem.

6. Role Play
OBJECTIVE: To write a group conversation; to combine verbal and non-verbal communication practice; to make group decisions.

- Read the instructions with the class and be sure the students understand them.
- Write a sample role play with the class and write it on the board. Act it out with volunteers.
- Divide the class into the suggested groupings.
- Have each group write their own role play.
- Circulate; help as needed.
- Have several groups present their role plays to the class.
- Have the students copy new words and phrases into the **Vocabulary** section of their notebooks.
- Discuss any topics that arise during the presentations.

7. Survey
OBJECTIVE: To learn about taking a survey and drawing conclusions from its results; to practice new vocabulary in an information gap activity.

- Model the questions; have students repeat; check pronunciation.
- Be sure students understand the vocabulary and the objectives of the survey.
- Vertically list the questions. Copy the horizontal part of the survey (YES/NO; ALWAYS/SOMETIMES/NEVER, etc.) on the board.
- Divide the class into the suggested groupings.
- Have students first check off their own answers in the appropriate column.
- Demonstrate the counting method by marking scores (///) under each heading. The fifth score is counted by a slash through the first four (7///)
- Have each group appoint a *leader* to ask the questions and a *recorder* to count the votes. As students raise their hands in response to each question the leader asks, the recorder counts the votes and announces the total to the group. Everyone then writes the correct number in the space provided.
- After the groups finish, ask leaders to report their results for each question. Have a student write the numbers reported on the board for each question and add them.
- Talk about the results. Draw conclusions.

8. What's the Story?
OBJECTIVE: To write a story using the creativity of all group members.

- Have students first read the directions and look at the illustrations, if applicable.
- Divide the class into the suggested groupings.
- Have each group select a *recorder* to write everyone's sentences.
- Encourage students to help each other. Try to have even the reluctant or shy students participating by contributing their sentences. Or have one of those students be the recorder.
- Have each group compose a story.
- After the stories are written, have all groups listen to their recorder read the story. Then have them make changes and corrections and edit their story. Give each

group time to decide whether their recorder will read the story or whether each student will read his or her sentences in turn.

- Photocopy the stories and distribute them in the next class for students to read. With the class, decide on the best story.

Partner Activities

1. Games

Pantomimes

- See Pantomimes in Group Activities.

Same or Different
OBJECTIVE: To practice observation skills and remembering detail.

- Explain the activity to the class. Do a few examples for practice.
- Divide the class into pairs.
- When all pairs have completed the activity, have several pairs report their results to the class.
- Take notes on the board. Who had the longest list?

What do you remember?
OBJECTIVE: To test observation and practice remembering detail.

- Talk about ways for the students to remember the details of the picture. Then have students close their texts.
- Divide the class into pairs.
- Have the pairs look at the illustration again briefly, discuss it, then close their texts.
- Have partners list everything they can remember together about the illustration.
- As partners complete the task, pair the partner groups so there are groups of four. Have the groups compare notes and amend their lists.
- Have groups report what they remember about the illustration to the class.
- Give each group a letter name and on the board write the number of details they had next to the letter. For example, if group A had eight items, write A-8; if B had six, write B-6.
- Show the transparency or have students look at the illustration in their texts. Have students add to their lists.
- Which group of four had the most detail?

2. Interview

OBJECTIVE: To practice asking, answering and listening to answers about a partner's experience; to report to the class.

- Model the questions first.
- Use a more confident student as your partner, or model both roles yourself.
- Practice the interview questions with the students. Be sure they understand the questions and the vocabulary. Check pronunciation. Supply any additional words needed.
- Teach conventions such as "Can you please repeat that?" or "I'm sorry; I don't understand." Also teach conventions for checking understanding such as "Do you mean . . . ?" or "Let me repeat what you said . . ."
- Divide the class into pairs.
- Have students write their partner's name in the space provided.
- Have students interview their partners. Remind them to ask their partners all the questions.
- Circulate; help as needed.
- Have several pairs present their interviews to the class.
- Write new vocabulary generated on the board.
- Have students copy the new words into the **Vocabulary** section of their notebooks.
- Use the students' responses to the interviews for further discussions.

3. Role Play
OBJECTIVE: To practice writing and role playing a different person; to review new vocabulary and structures in a given context.

- Set the scene. Have students imagine they are in the given situation.
- Explain that students will choose roles, write a conversation and then present it to the class.
- Some role plays are partial conversations. Read them together and be sure students understand. Check for pronunciation. Explain what kinds of phrases are needed to fit into the blanks.
- If necessary, write a sample role play on the board together with the class.
- Give students time to complete their role play conversation and practice it.
- Circulate; help as needed.
- Have several students present their role play to the class.
- Write new vocabulary on the board. Have students copy the new vocabulary into the **Vocabulary** section of their notebooks.

Individual Activities
1. Draw
OBJECTIVE: To depict a concept based on observation in a drawing; to talk about one's work.

- Model on the board what is expected from this activity.
- Give students enough time to complete their drawing.
- Circulate; help as needed, but also scout students who are particularly skilled in drawing and will be able to share a useful drawing—either on the board, on a transparency, or on photocopies.
- Use your own artwork too—the worse it is, sometimes the better. Students will be less reluctant to share theirs if yours isn't good!
- Have students discuss what they drew. Note new vocabulary words for them to copy into the **Vocabulary** section of their notebooks.

2. Speech
OBJECTIVE: To address a large group; to use vocabulary and structures.

- Make copies of the SPEECH and AUDIENCE EVALUATION forms in the **student text APPENDIX.**
- Read the instructions aloud.
- Write the outline for a very brief speech on the board. Explain how to write an outline rather than writing out every word.
- Model the speech. Make students aware of the time limit.
- Have students prepare speeches at home.
- Help students correct their speeches. Suggest they prepare note cards so they won't be reading the speeches. Help them limit their speech to the time limit.
- Have students practice their speech with you or in groups of four or five. Have the listeners give helpful hints on how to improve the speech. Give some hints yourself. Always phrase feedback in a positive way to encourage students and boost their confidence and self-esteem.
- Assign different students to be *evaluators* for different speakers.
- Distribute and review the forms. Be sure students understand how to use them.
- Collect the evaluations at the end of the class.
- Review the evaluations, add comments, and return them to the speakers. Discuss the evaluations in the next class, if appropriate.
- Remember to applaud all speeches!

3. Tell the Class
OBJECTIVE: To address a large group; to express information in an informal manner.

- Ask several students to volunteer a brief explanation of the particular activity.
- Since this is an informal report, don't dwell on corrections. Have as many students as possible participate.

- Encourage students to bring in visual aids, such as photos, postcards, etc.
- With the class, make displays of the items the students have brought to class. Have students write appropriate labels or captions.

4. Write (Journal)

OBJECTIVE: To learn how to keep a journal; to transfer oral information to written form.

- Review the questions with the students orally.
- If necessary, do some examples on the board so students understand the task.
- Divide the class into pairs.
- Have students write their partner's name in the space provided.
- Have partners interview their partners.
- Allow time for students to write in their journals.
- Circulate; help as needed.
- Have students read from their journals—either to their partners or to the class.
- Throughout the term, have students write journal entries in the **Journal** section of their notebooks. Minimize corrections; this activity is for fluency practice.

OBJECTIVES

The following is a checklist of topics, objectives, and skills covered in **A CONVERSATION BOOK 1**, **1A**, and **1B**.

LANGUAGE SKILL OBJECTIVES

- ❏ demonstrate understanding of simple words and questions from familiar material such as personal information and the immediate physical setting
- ❏ demonstrate comprehension of simple words in context of everyday situations
- ❏ demonstrate understanding of simple face-to-face conversations using previously learned material
- ❏ ask simple questions
- ❏ answer simple questions with yes, no, one word, or short phrase response
- ❏ communicate simple personal information
- ❏ participate in simple face-to-face conversations dealing with survival needs and minimum courtesy requirements
- ❏ respond appropriately to short emergency warnings
- ❏ demonstrate understanding of simple words and phrases drawn from learned topics
- ❏ demonstrate strategies to check for understanding and clarifying by attempting to reproduce what has been heard

LANGUAGE FUNCTIONS

- ❏ Identify
- ❏ Greet
- ❏ Introduce
- ❏ Demonstrate
- ❏ Show gratitude
- ❏ Caution
- ❏ Express state of being
- ❏ Command
- ❏ Request

- ❏ Agree/disagree
- ❏ Express satisfaction/ dissatisfaction
- ❏ Tell stories
- ❏ Take leave
- ❏ Ask for/report information
- ❏ Compliment
- ❏ Describe

- ❏ Express preference
- ❏ Invite
- ❏ Express necessity
- ❏ Express wants/desires
- ❏ Ask permission
- ❏ Follow directions
- ❏ Ask for/give directions
- ❏ Sequence

LANGUAGE FORMS

- ❏ simple commands
- ❏ affirmative/negative simple statements
- ❏ yes, no, wh- questions
- ❏ compound sentences with *and* and *but*

- ❏ Adverbial clauses of time
- ❏ possessives
- ❏ count/non-count
- ❏ adjectives
- ❏ how much/how many

- ❏ subject pronouns
- ❏ object pronouns
- ❏ prepositions of place
- ❏ articles
- ❏ demonstratives

VERB TENSES

- ❏ simple present tense: affirmative/negative question form
- ❏ simple past

- ❏ present continuous
- ❏ future
- ❏ modal: can
- ❏ future: will, going to

- ❏ modal: have to, should, must, may, would, could
- ❏ verbs + infinitives

GENERAL TOPICS

- ❏ personal information/ identification
- ❏ social communication
- ❏ family
- ❏ time
- ❏ weather
- ❏ money

- ❏ housing
- ❏ transportation
- ❏ emergencies
- ❏ general health
- ❏ medicine labels
- ❏ food: recipes/restaurants/ shopping/meals

- ❏ consumerism
- ❏ banking
- ❏ post office
- ❏ community resources
- ❏ school
- ❏ leisure

VOCATIONAL TOPICS

- ❏ job titles
- ❏ following instructions
- ❏ job skills
- ❏ classified ads
- ❏ job safety

- ❏ paychecks
- ❏ job applications
- ❏ job search strategies
- ❏ work schedules
- ❏ benefits

- ❏ clothing for work
- ❏ wages and deductions
- ❏ job interviews
- ❏ social security

A CONVERSATION BOOK 1
English in Everyday Life
Revised Third Edition

TEACHER'S GUIDE

UNIT 1

WELCOME TO CLASS

LEARNING STRATEGIES

➤ Introduce yourself to your classmates. Learn their names and your teacher's name. Write them down. After class, introduce yourself to other speakers and learners of English.

➤ Start a notebook. Divide it into sections:
Vocabulary
Activities
Journal
Community Information

WELCOME TO CLASS!

WARM UP

On the first day of class, set a supportive learning atmosphere. Use some of the suggestions in **NOTES TO THE TEACHER** in the **student text** or use your own ideas to welcome students.

- Use the first class as an icebreaker. Be informal and friendly.
- Provide name tags for all students, either only first names or first and last names.
- Spend time talking to students as they arrive.
- Don't feel compelled to use the book at all. You might use it only during the last half of the class.
- Use yourself as a model. If any students are slightly more fluent than the others, use the fluent students as models too.
- Introduce yourself. Speak slowly. Ask *What's your name?* Write *What's your name?* on the board. Write your name underneath. If a student doesn't understand, use another student as a model, or use yourself: ask yourself the question and then answer it.
- *Variation:* Use a hand or finger puppet. Ask the puppet questions and have the puppet answer. The puppet will help clarify the difference between the question and the answer.
- Ask information questions such as *What language do you speak?* or *Where do you live?* or *Where are you from?*
- Always model the question and answer both in writing and orally. If students want to copy from the board, give them time to do so.

IN THE TEXT

Draw

OBJECTIVE: To get acquainted through words and drawings.

- Make a frame on the board. Draw a picture of yourself. (Sometimes the *worse* your drawing is, the *more comfortable* students feel doing this activity!)
- Introduce yourself again; say your name. Describe your picture using the vocabulary in the text.
- *Variation:* Have students describe the picture; on the board list the vocabulary they generate.
- Illustrate the vocabulary and clarify any concepts with drawings on the board, or with the students themselves. For example, use a student with a mustache to explain the word.
- Ask students if they can add other descriptive words and list these on the board. Students may need help in finding the words they need.
- *Variation:* Fill in this section during **Tell the Class.**
- Have students take a few minutes and draw pictures of themselves.
- *Variation:* Have them draw a picture of a partner.

Write

OBJECTIVE: To transfer oral information to written form.

- Go over this section orally first. If you haven't used it to describe your own picture on the board, do so now.

- Have students write their answers.
- Circulate; help as needed.

Tell the Class

OBJECTIVE: To use vocabulary to describe self-portraits.

- Ask several students to describe their pictures.
- Instruct the student to write his/her name on the board first, and then to show his/her picture to the class and describe it, using the guidelines from **Write** on page 2 in the **student text**.
- Be sure to compliment those students who are "brave" enough to volunteer—or be volunteered. Don't dwell on corrections.
- Ask individual students what they wish to be called in class. See **Names/Nicknames** in the **student text APPENDIX** on page 246 if appropriate.

Partner Activity

OBJECTIVE: To introduce oneself and respond correctly.

- Model the conversation. Use a confident student as your partner, or do both A and B yourself for the model.
- *Variation:* Draw A and B stick figures on the board to clarify that two people are speaking. Or use puppets.
- Divide the class into pairs. There are suggestions for pairing in **GROUPING** on page xvi in **TO THE TEACHER** in the **student text**. Always pair students with a method suitable for your classroom situation.
- Have students practice the conversation, filling in their names.
- Give several students the opportunity to present their partners to the class.
- Ask the class to respond with one of the appropriate replies: *Nice to meet you; I'm pleased to meet you.*

Group Activity

OBJECTIVE: To review names and vocabulary relating to introductions.

- Divide the class into groups of three or four.
- Instruct students to write their first names on name cards. Then have each student pronounce his or her name and have others repeat it. Then have each student introduce himself or herself to the group, using the phrases from the **Partner Activity**.

EXPANSION

- Have students take turns writing their names on the board. Take advantage of the cross-cultural nature of this activity. (For example, in some cultures, last names are written first.)
- Explain how names are given and used in the United States and Canada. (The order is first, middle, last. When a woman gets married, she usually, but not always, takes her husband's last name. Sometimes people hyphenate names.)
- Talk about names and nicknames. (See the **student text APPENDIX, Names/Nicknames**, page 246.) Ask *What names are popular in your countries? Are nicknames popular? What nicknames are popular?*
- Write the names and nicknames on the board for students to see.

COUNTRIES

WARM UP

- Post a large world map or show the transparency. Point to the place where you are now.
- Have different students come to the map, tell where they are from, and point to the place. Ask *Where are you from?* If all the students are from the same country, ask *What city are you from?*
- Point to the different countries. Ask what they are. Write the names on the board as students tell you what to write.
- Ask about oceans: *What ocean is near England?* or *What oceans are near the United States and Canada?*
- Expand with major cities. Ask *What is the capital of France?* or *What is the capital of Japan?*

IN THE TEXT

- To introduce the vocabulary, see the suggested procedures in **TO THE TEACHER**.
- Use phrases again such as *Where are you from?* and *Where is Japan?* and *What ocean is near Brazil?*

Class Activity

OBJECTIVE: To locate places on a map.

- Tell students to circle their home countries or cities on the map. Have them do the same for their classmates' home countries or cities.

Partner Interview

OBJECTIVE: To ask, answer, and listen to answers about a partner's experience; to report answers.

- Model the conversation first. Use a more confident student as your partner, or model both roles yourself.
- Practice the interview questions with all the students. Be sure they understand the questions and the vocabulary. Check pronunciation. Supply any additional words needed.
- Divide the class into pairs.
- Have students interview their partners. Remind them to ask their partners all of the questions.
- Circulate; help as needed.
- Have several pairs present their interviews to the class.
- Write the new vocabulary generated on the board.
- Have students copy the new words into the **Vocabulary** section of their notebooks.
- Use the students' responses to the interviews for further discussions.

Tell the Class

OBJECTIVE: To process information; to address a large group.

- Ask one partner from several pairs to tell the class about their partners. Have them make an introduction. Model *I'd like you to meet Juan. He is from Cali, Colombia. Colombia is in South America. He lives in Lawrence now. He speaks Spanish and a little English.*

Class Game: *"Where do you want to visit?"*

OBJECTIVE: To associate words with actions; to reinforce names of other students.

This is a modified TPR [Total Physical Response] game. This type of game appears throughout the text, but it is illustrated only on page 5. Here, students learn the actions through illustration, words and movement.

- Give out slips of paper to each student.
- Model all the actions with exaggerated motions.
    Think: Show yourself thinking of something. (In this case, think of a place. Look at the map on the transparency or in the text. See the **student text APPENDIX, Maps**, pages 240–244, for reference, if appropriate.)
    Write the name of a place (such as **Madrid**) on a slip of paper.
- Use a dark marking pen. Hold it up for the class to see.
- Have students write a place they would like to visit on their slips of paper.
    Fold your paper. Have students fold their papers.
    Make a pile: Put your folded paper on your desk. Have students come up and put their folded papers on top of yours. The papers should form a pile. Shuffle the pile of papers.
    Open the first one. Read it.
    Guess: (Model guessing) *I think Emi wants to go to Cuba.* If you are wrong, have students guess who wrote the slip of paper.
- Whoever guesses the correct name gets to pick the next slip.
- As students are named, they should indicate their "place" on the large map or on the transparency.

Tell the Class

OBJECTIVE: To process information and to address a large group; to express preferences.

- Have several students tell the class what place they want to visit and tell why they want to visit that place. (When students volunteer for this activity, it will allow you to assess their confidence and willingness to speak. Remember, some students may not yet be ready to recite to the class.)

EXPANSION

- Encourage students to bring in pictures, postcards and other realia from their countries. Have a "Show and Tell" session.
- Make a bulletin board with the items. Attach labels with the names of the students and the places.

- •• Play "Geography" with the class. Say the name of a continent or country (**Korea**, for example). The first student names a city, a state, a country, or a continent starting with the last letter of Africa (**Athens**). The next student does the same (**Sicily**). Follow this pattern around the circle or the room (**Yugoslavia**). If someone can't name a place, he or she is "out" of this round.
- You can play this game as a class or in teams, with students helping each other think of names.

NUMBERS

WARM UP

- Introduce the page on numbers by writing the numbers 1–10 on the board. See if students can call out the number as you point to it, first in order, then randomly.
- Do the same with the numbers to 100.
- Write *How many?* on the board. Introduce the question *How many?* by using objects around the classroom. For example, ask *How many books do I have?* or *How many windows are in the classroom?*
- Ask questions that require students to understand and raise their hands in response, such as *How many students have children?* Have the class count the raised hands out loud.

IN THE TEXT

- To introduce the vocabulary, see the suggested procedures in **TO THE TEACHER.**
- Expand 30s, 40s, 50s, and so on (31, 32, 33, . . .).

Class Survey

OBJECTIVE: To reinforce vocabulary by counting and observing classmates.

- Copy the chart from the **student text** onto the board. Write abbreviated questions.
- Tell the class they need to count to answer the questions.
- Read the directions in the text together.
- After the class finishes counting, ask for their answers and fill in the chart on the board.
- If answers disagree, have students raise their hands as you ask the questions again. Count out loud. Have students count with you.
- Write any new vocabulary on the board. Have students copy the new words into the **Vocabulary** section of their notebooks.

Group Activity

OBJECTIVE: To review what classmates have learned about classmates.

- Read the instructions in the text together. Divide the class into groups of four.
- After group members have compared their individual lists, have one member of each group read a list of someone in the group to the class. The class has to guess who it is. Have each group take a turn.

EXPANSION

- Dictation: Have students write the number words as you dictate them in random order.
- • If students can discuss numbers and superstition, talk about different numbers and cultures. Why is 13 an unlucky number in the United States and Canada? Are there lucky and unlucky numbers in other cultures?

JOURNAL

WARM UP

- Tell the class that all students will be keeping journals for this course in their own notebooks. Explain that a journal is a record of thoughts and experiences kept on a daily or weekly (or in this case, unit) basis. The journals will be very guided, and the vocabulary will generally be a review of the vocabulary introduced and used in each unit.
- This journal will serve as a review of the first three pages of this unit. Explain the process; students will interview each other first and then write about their interviews.

IN THE TEXT

Partner Interview

- Follow the suggested procedures on page T4.

Write

OBJECTIVE: To learn how to keep a journal and to write the first journal entry; to transfer oral information to written form.

- Have students do their individual journal writing in their texts.
- Circulate; help as needed.

Tell the Class

OBJECTIVE: To process information; to address a large group.

- Have several students read their journal entries to the class.
- On the board, write the skeleton journal paragraph as it appears in the text.
- *Variation:* Use the transparency instead of writing on the board. Either you or the students can fill in the blanks.
- Ask students to read aloud what they wrote on the board or on the transparency. Or you can read it as a model.

EXPANSION

- If students like journal writing, have them write their own entries in the **Journal** section of their notebooks on a daily or weekly basis. Provide models and skeleton paragraphs at first.

- •• Use several journals for dictation practice. Discuss conventions of writing (for example, sentences, paragraphs, dates, mechanics of punctuation).

CLOTHING AND COLORS

WARM UP

- Admire a few students' shirts, blouses, or dresses. Talk about the colors.
- Talk about what you are wearing in a "Show and Tell." For example, point out your jacket. Include the pockets or buttons, etc., as you speak. *Today I'm wearing my favorite jacket. It's black cotton. I like it because it's comfortable and it has pockets. The four buttons are white.* Ask students to describe what they are wearing. Write the vocabulary they elicit on the board.
- Review the present continuous tense in **Grammar for Conversation**, page 220 of the **student text**.

IN THE TEXT

- To introduce vocabulary, see the suggested procedures in **TO THE TEACHER**.
- Ask students what articles of clothing they already know the words for.
- Teach vocabulary of colors by using the items in the illustration, clothing worn by the class and by you, as well as objects around the room.
- How many of these items does the class have on today? Ask questions such as *Who is wearing a skirt today? Who is wearing green today?* and write the answers on the board. *Mary is wearing a green skirt, José is wearing a yellow sweatshirt,* etc. Point out the two types of jackets: sports coat and outer jacket.
- Ask students if they can add other words to the list. Write them on the board for everyone to copy into their texts.

Partner Game: *"What do you remember?"*

OBJECTIVE: To test observation and to practice clothing vocabulary.

- Divide the class into pairs. Partners are going to make a list of each other's clothes. Have them take a moment to look at their partner.
- Have partners sit back to back and list each other's clothing—without looking!
- Ask partners to read their lists to each other and correct their lists.
- *Variation:* Have several pairs read their lists to the class without turning around. The class then corrects the list.
- Write new words on the board for the students to copy into the **Vocabulary** section of their notebooks.

Class Activity

OBJECTIVE: To review colors and counting; to add new vocabulary.

- Have the class dictate the colors everyone in the class is wearing.
- Write the colors on the board in a vertical list.
- Make horizontal columns on the board for MEN and WOMEN.
- Have the class count the number of men and women wearing each color. Have a student write the numbers on the board. Include yourself!
- Have the class "vote" on their favorite color.

EXPANSION

- Discuss the fabrics of the clothing students are wearing.

PAIRS OF CLOTHING

WARM UP

- If the topic of **pairs** hasn't come up in the previous lesson, introduce the concept. Point out shoes, earrings, or glasses on yourself or on different students. Emphasize the words *pair of*.
- Ask if students can name pairs of things without looking at the illustration. List their suggestions on the board. (Underwear should be handled according to your own judgment—it is important vocabulary for students to know, but it may be an inappropriate topic, depending on the class.)

IN THE TEXT

- To introduce vocabulary, see the suggested procedures in **TO THE TEACHER**.

Group Game: *"True or false?"*
OBJECTIVE: To learn to discriminate between true and false statements.

- Explain the words "true" and "false."
- Make statements about clothing, such as *I'm wearing purple shoes.* Have students say *true* or *false*. Practice several examples.
- Divide students into groups of four. Have them write three true statements about their clothes and one false statement in the **Activity** section of their notebooks.
- Have students take turns reading their statements. Other students in the group should decide which statement is false.
- Have each group select one *reporter* to read one of the group's statements to the class. The class then has to decide on the false statement and guess which student wrote it.

Group Game: *"What am I wearing?"*
OBJECTIVE: To describe articles of clothing.

- Have each group of four above secretly pick a student from another group and write a description of that person's clothing.
- Have the *reporter* from the group read the description to the class. Ask the class to guess who it is!

EXPANSION

- Make index cards for *matching* items (for example, one card for GREEN, and another for GRASS; one for BLUE and another for SKY; YELLOW/SUN; RED/APPLE). Be sure students understand the new vocabulary.
- Give each student a card; have them circulate around the room and find the match. As soon as they do, they may sit down.
- Have several pairs read their cards. Use this technique for pairing from time to time.

FAMILY

WARM UP

- Bring in photos of your own family and illustrations from magazines, newspapers, or your picture file.
- First talk to the students about the families depicted in the magazines and newspapers; who is who? Write the new vocabulary words on the board.
- Then talk to the students about your own family. This personalization will encourage students to talk about their families.

IN THE TEXT

- To introduce the vocabulary, see the suggested procedures in **TO THE TEACHER.**
- Take each frame separately. Model the vocabulary as you point to each corresponding illustration.
- Ask questions as appropriate. *Do you have any sisters or brothers?* or *How many sisters do you have? How many brothers?* etc.
- Ask about names. *What is your mother's name?* etc.
- Explain the concept of *single parent, in-laws,* and *pets.*
- Ask about family relationships in students' cultures. *Are large families common? Do families live together or close by? Do people have pets?* etc.
- Have students talk about the family in the illustrations. *What are their names? What do they do?* etc.

Tell the Class

OBJECTIVE: To describe characteristics of a favorite person; to address a large group.

- Model this activity. Tell the class about a favorite person you know. *My grandmother is my favorite person. She is old. She has gray hair. She is a little heavy. She is kind, understanding, and patient. All the children in the family love her. The adults love her, too.*
- Create another paragraph with a student who volunteers. Write the paragraph on the board. Be sure students understand the new vocabulary.
- Divide the class into groups of four or five. Have them tell each other about a favorite person.
- Circulate; help as needed.
- Have the groups decide on the story they like best; have that student describe his or her favorite person to the entire class.
- Write any new vocabulary on the board. Have students copy the new words into the **Vocabulary** section of their notebooks.

Partner Interview

- Follow the suggested procedures on page T4.

Draw

OBJECTIVE: To think through family relationships and physical characteristics and to depict them through words and drawings.

- Draw your own rough family portrait or family tree on the board.
- Explain it to the class.
- Give students time to draw their families or their family trees.

- Circulate; help as needed.
- Have students show their family portraits or family trees and explain them to their group. Have one student from each group explain his or her drawing to the class.

Tell the Class

OBJECTIVE: To use vocabulary and familiar photographs to talk about families; to address a large group.

- As an assignment for the next class, have students bring in photos of their families.
- Let students show the class the photos and tell the class about their families.

EXPANSION

- Either create another bulletin board or take down the cards from **EXPANSION**, page T5. Put up the students' photos. Have students label the photos to tell *Who, Where, and When.*

●● Students might like to give names to the people on page 10; these people will be appearing throughout the text. Have students decide their names, ages, where they live, the names of their pets, etc.

●●● Have students write a paragraph about their own favorite family member.

REVIEW

IN THE TEXT

Partner Interview

- Follow the suggested procedures on page T4.

Find Someone Who

OBJECTIVE: To ask yes/no questions; to share personal information with classmates.

- Review the vocabulary.
- To demonstrate how to create the yes/no questions, write a sample question on the board: *Do you speak three languages?* Ask individual students the question until you get a "yes" answer. Then write the completed sentence on the board. (*1. Han Lee speaks three languages.*)
- Repeat this procedure for the other questions. Be sure students understand all the vocabulary.
- If appropriate, review grammatical structures at this point.
- Have students circulate around the room and ask each question. If the class is very large, break it into groups of 10–15 and have them do the activity within their groups.
- When students find a "yes" answer, instruct them to write that student's name in the space.
- When students have completed the activity, have them sit in their seats.
- Call on individual students to give you the answers to the questions.
- Take advantage of interesting information about the class that gets generated from this activity.

EXPANSION

- Review all illustrations in the unit or show the transparencies from **Unit 1** again.
- Have students list as many vocabulary words as they can remember without looking back in their books.
- Have students compare notes, either in small groups or as a class.

UNIT TEST

- A **conversation test** and a **vocabulary test** for this unit are located in the back of this Teacher's Guide, plus suggestions for administration. Feel free to make as many copies as you need.

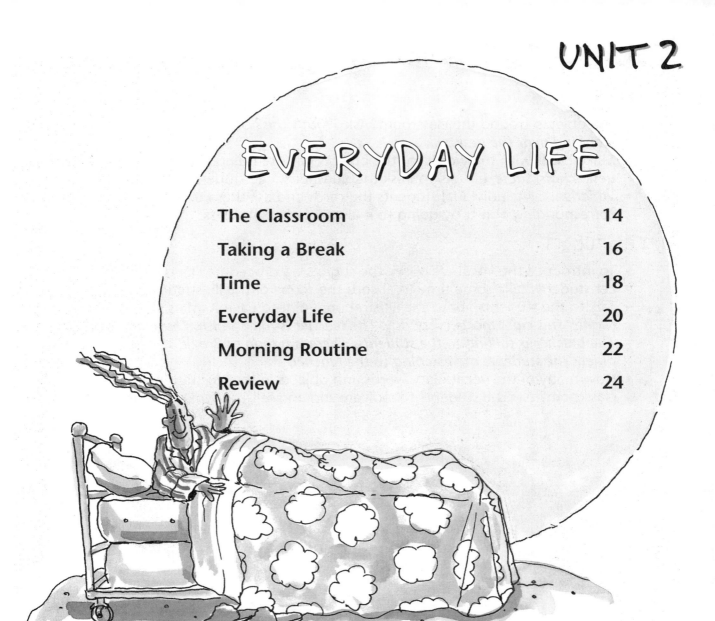

EVERYDAY LIFE

LEARNING STRATEGIES

➤ Make vocabulary cards for new words. Study the cards every day. Memorize five new words every day.

➤ Talk in English with a classmate on your break every day.

THE CLASSROOM

WARM UP

- Use objects around the classroom. Ask **What's this?** or make a statement such as **I'm standing near the desk.**
- Make cards with the words for the objects you are going to teach: **window, door, desk, chair, table,** etc. As you ask the questions, cue students with the card.
- *Variation:* Give individual students the cards and ask them to match the corresponding object by going to it and showing the class.

IN THE TEXT

- To introduce the vocabulary, see the suggested procedures in **TO THE TEACHER.**
- Let students take some time to absorb the scope of the illustration.
- Talk to the students about the illustration. Point to each item as you use the word. Model **This class meets every day. The teacher is Alice Smith. There are eight students. The teacher is talking to the students. There is a map of Brazil. It is 8:00. The class is quiet. The students are listening to the teacher.**
- How many of the vocabulary words and objects in the illustration are in *your* classroom? Ask the students to look around and tell you what they are.

Draw

OBJECTIVE: To observe items in the classroom; to associate the objects with their English names, and to depict them through words and drawings.

- Have students look around the room for a minute.
- In the space provided, students should draw, as best they can, the things in the room and label each object. Demonstrate by drawing a desk on the board and labeling it.
- Have students count how many items they drew and put that number on the picture.
- Have them circle the number. Model this on the board.
- Have them find partners and compare their drawings with the partner, adding the things they forgot.
- Ask students how many items they originally drew. Who had the most?
- *Variation:* Divide the class into teams of three or four. Have each team collaborate and draw one picture of the classroom on a separate piece of paper. Give the teams ten minutes to complete their drawings. Collect the drawings. Make transparencies or copies.
- In the next class, show the transparencies or hand out the copies. Have the class select the most complete one.

Group Game: *"What is it?"*

OBJECTIVE: To integrate vocabulary and ask yes/no questions about the classroom through an information-gap activity.

- This is a simplified form of "20 Questions," but there is no set limit to the number of questions students can ask.
- Read the instructions aloud with the students.
- Demonstrate possible yes/no questions (*Is it green? Is it small?*). Write these questions on the board.
- Have students suggest other yes/no questions. (This should elicit words such as *big, little, round, square,* etc.) Add them to the list on the board.
- You be the *leader* first. Say *I'm thinking of something in the classroom. It's white.*
- Students have to ask you yes/no questions.
- When a student guesses the correct word, that student becomes the new leader and the game continues.
- Now divide the class into groups of six and have them play the game.
- Review any new vocabulary and write it on the board. Have students copy the new words into the **Vocabulary** section of their notebooks.

EXPANSION

- Create a story with the students about one of the students in the illustration on page 15. Write their story on the board as they dictate it. For example, point to a woman and ask:

What's her name?
Where is she from?
Where does she live now?
What does she look like?
What is she doing?
What colors are her clothes?
Does she like her English class?

TAKING A BREAK

WARM UP

- Do you give breaks during class? What do you do? What do the students do? On the board list the things you and the students do during a break.

IN THE TEXT

- Look at the illustration with the students or show the transparency with books closed.
- Tell a story about the illustration. For example, ***This class is very noisy. They are taking a break. Look at this student.*** (Point to the student who is sleeping.) ***He's tired. He's sleeping.*** (Point) ***These students are reading.*** (Point) ***This student is waving to a friend.*** (Point) ***Here's another student. He's thirsty. He's having a cold drink. What do you think it is?*** (Point) ***Look at the teacher. She's talking to a student. What do you think they are talking about?*** Etc.
- Have students as involved as possible as you make up the story.
- *Variation:* Do a pantomime activity. Choose a word and act it out. Say ***What am I doing?*** or ***How am I today?***
- Have students call out the right word. Or have students call out an action and pantomime it. Make mistakes. Have them correct you by saying the word and acting it out. Choose another leader and continue.
- After you have discussed the illustration, follow the suggested procedures in **TO THE TEACHER**.
- The activities in this lesson call for the present continuous tense, the verb *to be* present tense, and present tense of other verbs. This is a good opportunity to review these tenses in **Grammar for Conversation**, pages 219–220 in the **student text**.

Class Game: *"What am I doing?"*

OBJECTIVE: To associate words with actions; to reinforce names of students.

- The steps to this activity are illustrated on **student text** page 5. You may want to refer back.
- Prepare students by giving out slips of paper for them to write an activity.
- Model all instructions in exaggerated motions. Have students follow your lead and do the action as you did.
- Have the students guess what you and they are doing.
- To review, have a student read the actions and have the class follow the instruction.
- *Variation:* Have half of the class read and the other half respond with the action.

Partner Game: *"How are you today?"*

OBJECTIVE: To decide about feelings and moods; to answer the questions *How are you? How is he or she today?*

- Have partners look at all the illustrations and decide how the people are. Have them fill in the balloon for the mascot (**your own**).
- Circulate; help as needed.
- When all pairs have finished, have them report back to the class. Compare answers. Ask why they made their decisions. Ask why they are feeling as they described.
- *Variation:* As partners are working, write the nine adjectives on the board. Have students suggest other adjectives. Write them on the board for everyone to copy into their texts.
- Ask how many of the students in the picture are *happy, sick, tired,* etc. If there is disagreement, have students tell you why they chose a certain word over another.

Group Vocabulary Challenge

OBJECTIVE: To review the vocabulary of the lesson; to add new words to students' vocabulary.

- Divide the class into groups of four.
- Have each group select a *recorder*.
- Instruct students to make one list per group of all the things students and teachers can do during a break.
- Give students a specific time frame to work in, for example, ten minutes.
- Tell the recorders to write the list of words and expressions as students dictate them.
- When time is up, have each group's recorder read their list to the class.
- Compare lists. Which group has the longest list? the most new words?
- Have students copy the new words into the **Vocabulary** section of their notebooks.

EXPANSION

- With the students, create a story about the illustration on page 16.
- •• Divide students into groups.
- Have each group pick a student in the illustration and write a story about that student.
- Circulate; help as needed.

TIME

WARM UP

- Bring to class a clock that you can change times on (a paper plate with fastener hands still works well!).
- Ask students what time it is. If someone looks at his/her watch, admire it—write the word *watch* on the board. Ask about the watch. ***What kind of watch is it? What color is it? Do you like the watch?*** etc.
- Put a rough picture of the sun on the board. This indicates daylight hours. Draw a stick figure of a person eating breakfast. Draw a clock that says 7:00. Ask ***What time is it?***
- Introduce the words ***breakfast, morning, a.m.***
- Do similar drawings and clocks for ***lunch, dinner, going to bed, waking up, afternoon, evening, night, p.m.,*** etc. (Use a picture of the moon and stars to indicate evening and night.)
- Show a clock. Talk about the time: the hour hand, minute hand, second hand.
- If you have a clock with moveable hands, practice making different times and asking students what time it is. Have a student place a time, and ask the class what time it is. Put any key phrases such as ***What time is it?*** and ***It's _____*** on the board.
- Set the clock to show 3:15, then 3:50; 7:14, 7:40; 6:13, 6:30. Practice pronouncing and listening to the differences.
- Write the similar sets on the board; say one and see if students can identify what you said. Teach ***to, past, of, after.*** Write different ways to say the same time on the board, and have students copy these phrases into the **Vocabulary** section of their notebooks.

IN THE TEXT

- Look at the illustrations on pages 18 and 19 with the students or show the transparency with books closed.
- Narrate the story of the student for the class. Use as many words from the vocabulary list as you can.
- If there is too much vocabulary, take a single frame at a time; name the student, tell the story, put the key words on the board.

Class Discussion

OBJECTIVE: To integrate new vocabulary; to learn to narrate a story.

- Have students tell you the story, frame by frame. Ask questions such as ***What time does he eat breakfast? go to school?*** etc.
- As you tell the story, point out the variation in clocks: ***digital, analog*** (one with hands), ***watches, alarm clocks.*** Ask students if they have clocks like these. Can they mention—or draw—other types of clocks?
- You may want to clarify verb usage. Point out contrast between present continuous and simple present tense. (***It's 6:00. He is getting up. He gets up at 6:00 every day.***)

Partner Interview

- Follow the suggested procedures on T4.

Group Survey

OBJECTIVE: To learn about taking a survey and drawing conclusions from its results; to practice new vocabulary in an information gap activity.

- Model the questions; have students repeat; check pronunciation.
- Be sure students understand the vocabulary and the objective.
- Copy the chart from the **student text** on the board.
- Tell the class they are going to take part in a survey.
- Divide the class into small groups.
- Have students first check off their own answers in the appropriate column.
- Demonstrate the counting method by marking scores (///) under each heading. The fifth score is counted by a slash through the first four. (7///L)
- Have each group appoint a *leader* to ask the questions and a *recorder* to count the "votes." As students raise their hands in response to each question the leader asks, the recorder counts the votes and announces the total to the group. Everyone then writes the correct number in the space provided.
- After groups finish, ask each leader to report their results for each question. Have a student write the results for each question on the board and add them. Continue with all the questions.
- Talk about the results. Draw conclusions. What do most students do every day?

EXPANSION

- Use your picture file. Show students illustrations of different activities of the day. Ask what time they think it is. This can be done in a group, with the whole class, or with partners. If you do this in groups or with partners, give out the illustrations. Have students decide on the time and report back to the class.

- •• Make sets of matching cards or photocopied sheets. For example, make up a card or a sheet with the time *6:30 a.m.* and a matching card or sheet with either the words *wake up* or an illustration of someone waking up.

  Other possibilities:

7:00 a.m.	*eat breakfast*
8:00 a.m.	*go to work*
12:00 noon	*eat lunch*
6:00 p.m.	*have dinner with a friend*
11:00 p.m.	*go to bed*

- Make enough cards to give *two random cards* to each student.
- *Variation:* Make a duplicate set for each group of five or six students (two random cards for each student in the group).
- Have students match the time with the activity by working with other students in their group. After they have found their matches, have them put the activities and times together to tell a logical story. When they are finished, the class or the groups can tell the story, each student telling his or her time and activity.

EVERYDAY LIFE

WARM UP

- Use your picture file, or bring to class magazine or newspaper illustrations of some everyday activities relevant to the students and their community.
- Pose the question *What do you do every day?*
- If necessary, answer it yourself, using the illustrations to help define the vocabulary.
- Put words on the board. Include *time* expressions as a review.
- Draw stick figures on the board. Tell a story about what they do every day. Write the vocabulary next to each action.

IN THE TEXT

- Look at the illustrations with the students, or show the transparency with books closed.
- Show **A Mother's Day** first. Cover **A Worker's Day.**
- Have the students name the mother and the children. Tell the daily story of the mother as you point to each illustration. Write each action on the board as you talk about it (or write on the transparency itself). Model: (mother's name) *day starts very early in the morning—at* (students tell you) _____ *o'clock. First, she feeds* (baby's name) *because she is hungry. While* (baby's name) *is sleeping,* (mother's name) *sweeps the floor. Then she gets ready for school. Her English class is at* (students tell you) _____ *o'clock. After class, she goes shopping for her family. When she comes home, she cooks dinner for her family. Then she washes the dishes. After she finishes the dishes, she reads to* (children's names) *and puts them to bed. Then she does her homework. She has a long day!*
- Go over the story again. Have different students tell the story as you point to the vocabulary.
- *Variation:* Have students tell *you* the story. Help with vocabulary.
- Follow the same procedure for **A Worker's Day.**

Class Discussion

OBJECTIVE: To integrate new vocabulary; to compare and contrast.

- With the students, decide on appropriate times for each activity.
- Draw clocks on the board and fill them in as the class decides on the time.
- Have students copy the clock times into their texts.
- Ask students to compare the routines. What do the mother and the worker do that is similar? What is different? Make a list on the board, using the titles SAME and DIFFERENT. Explain these words.
- Give some examples:

SAME	DIFFERENT
1. They both go to school.	1. She goes to school in the morning; he goes to school at night.
2. They both do homework.	2. She studies at home; he studies at the laundromat.
	3. She lives with her family; he lives alone.

- Follow up with any discussion that arises from this activity.

Draw

OBJECTIVE: To integrate daily routine vocabulary into the context of personal experience; to depict daily routine through words and drawings.

- Talk about your own day. Use the examples from the **WARM UP**. Use other forms of realia such as a coffee mug, alarm clock, etc. For example, if you say *I have coffee in the morning*, show the coffee mug as a visual aid.
- Draw eight boxes on the board and draw stick figures to illustrate your day. Ask students what to write below the drawings.
- Ask students about their routine. Illustrate with stick figures or write the vocabulary on the board as the student tells you about his/her routine. For example,

Juanita	*Sam*
walks the dog	**goes to bed**
has breakfast	**has breakfast**
reads the newspaper	**studies**
goes to school	**picks up his son at school**
watches tv	**goes to work**

- You may want to clarify verb usage. Point out the contrast between the third person singular **–s** and the first person (no **-s**).
- List several students' routines on the board. Then ask another student *What does Juanita do every day?*
- Have the student use the vocabulary cues to tell the story.
- Have the class do the activity, drawing and making short statements about their day.
- Circulate around the room; help as needed.
- Give several students the chance to put some or all of their stories on the board, and have them tell the class about each box.

Partner Activity

OBJECTIVE: To talk about daily routines; to ask and answer questions and listen to a partner.

- Have students compare their day with their partner's. Have them list the similarities and differences. Write the titles SAME and DIFFERENT on the board.
- Use your example of a routine on the board. Ask a student to help you compare his or her routine with yours. Write the similarities and differences.
- Have partners do the activity. Have several partners report back to the class.

Find Someone Who

- Follow the suggested procedures on page T12.

EXPANSION

- Ask students about someone else's day (their mothers, their fathers, their wives, their husbands, their children, etc.).

- • Have them write a short paragraph about that person and read it to the class.

MORNING ROUTINE

WARM UP

- Bring in *morning routine* items, such as **an alarm clock, a coffee mug, a toothbrush, textbooks, the newspaper, orange juice**, etc.
- Line these things up on the table and have different students pick one and tell the class what it is and what they do with it in the morning.
- *Variation:* Have everything in a bag or box and have students pick randomly, then describe the article.
- Have students tell you a morning routine story using the items.

IN THE TEXT

- Look at the illustrations on both pages with the students or show the transparency with books closed.
- Tell the story about the man. Have the students name him. Ask **What is** (*Name*) **doing?** You may have to answer something like (*Name*) **is waking up early. He always wakes up early during the week.** Repeat this procedure for each frame. Use different adverbs of frequency. For example, **He is taking a shower. He takes a shower every day; He is singing in the shower. He usually sings in the shower.**
- Have students help you tell the story by asking either **What is he doing?** or **Is he having breakfast or leaving for work?** Then repeat, **Yes,** (*Name*) **is having breakfast now.** Students will catch on after you ask a few questions and answers.
- Continue with all vocabulary. Ask students if they can think of other *morning routine* vocabulary items. Write the words on the board; have students copy them into the spaces provided in their texts.
- You may want to review the –s for third person singular. Also, you may want to review the difference between the simple present tense and the present continuous. Talk about how adverbs of frequency can indicate tense.
- With the class, decide on captions for each frame. Write the captions on the board and have students copy them under the appropriate picture in their text.
- To introduce the vocabulary, see the suggested procedures in **TO THE TEACHER**.

What's the Story?

OBJECTIVE: To write a story using the creativity of all group members.

- First have students read the directions and look at the illustrations.
- Divide the class into groups of three.
- Have each group select a *recorder* to write everyone's sentences.
- Encourage students to help each other. Try to have even the reluctant or shy students participate by contributing their sentences. Or have one of those students be the recorder.
- Have each group write a story.
- After the stories are written, all groups should listen to their recorder read the story. They should all make changes and corrections and 'edit' their story. Each group should decide whether the recorder will read the story or whether each student will take turns reading his/her sentences.
- Photocopy the stories and distribute them in the next class for students to read.
- With the class, decide on the most creative story.

Group Game: *"What do you do in the morning?"*

OBJECTIVE: To associate words with actions; to practice gestures.

- Do a few practice pantomimes with the students.
- Divide the class into groups of five and have each student pantomime one activity. Have the others in the group guess the activity.
- Review with the whole class, if students need the practice.

EXPANSION

- Play a spelling game. Write on the board any word or phrase from the last two units. For example, *comb*. The next student in the chain has to think of a word beginning with *b*, such as *breakfast*. The next student thinks of a word beginning with *t*.
- Continue around the room.
- Write any new vocabulary words on the board.
- Have students copy the new words into the **Vocabulary** section of their notebooks.

REVIEW

IN THE TEXT

Group Vocabulary Challenge

- Follow the suggested procedures on page T17, but divide into groups of five rather than four.

Class Activity

OBJECTIVE: To practice posing questions about daily activities.

- With the class, brainstorm ten questions about daily and morning routines.
- Write the questions on the board as the class poses them.

Partner Activity

OBJECTIVE: To answer questions about daily activities.

- Divide the class into pairs.
- Have partners ask each other the questions written on the board. (It is best NOT to have them write anything, but they may have to for "prompts.")
- After partners have had the chance to practice the questions, have them present their interviews to the class.

Partner Game: *"What do you do every day?"*

OBJECTIVE: To associate words with actions.

- With the same partners, have students take turns pantomiming daily activities.
- Partners should decide on five of the activities to show to the class.
- Partner 1 should introduce the pantomime by saying something like *Miyako does these activities every day. Can you guess what they are?*
- Then Partner 2 acts out five activities and the class guesses the activities.
- Partners then reverse roles.

EXPANSION

- Review all illustrations in the unit, or show the transparencies from Unit 2 again.
- Have students make up questions about the illustrations. Write their questions on the board.
- Have individual students choose a question and ask either a specific student or anyone in the class.
- When that student answers, he/she asks the next question.

UNIT TEST

- A **conversation test** and a **vocabulary test** for this unit are located in the back of this Teacher's Guide, plus suggestions for administration. Feel free to make as many copies as you need.

THE CALENDAR

LEARNING STRATEGIES

➤ Make a calendar in English for this month. Write your activities on the calendar every day.

➤ In the Journal section of your notebook, write about the weather every day. For example, "Today the weather is . . ."

DAYS OF THE WEEK

WARM UP

- Use a large, simplified calendar to show days, dates, and numbers.
- You may want to clarify verb usage. Review contrast between simple present and present continuous. Point out uses of past tense and future with **going to**. Talk about today (*present continuous* and *simple present*), yesterday (*past tense*), and tomorrow (with *going to*). Refer to **Grammar for Conversation**, pages 219–220, 223–224, and 226 in the **student text**.
- Use as much vocabulary of the lesson as possible. For example, *Today is Monday. I am in our English class now. Yesterday was Sunday, and it was the weekend. Yesterday I visited my family. Tomorrow is a busy day. It is Tuesday. I'm going to work in the morning. In the afternoon I'm going shopping. Then I'm going to have dinner with a friend,* etc. (Make your narrative as short or long, simple or complex as the class' level will allow. Use as many of the words that they have learned as possible.)
- Show pictures from your picture file to help with comprehension.
- Ask students what they are doing today. Point to the day.
- *Variation:* For a more simple **WARM UP**, ask questions (don't require full sentences; the objective is comprehension) such as the following:

  What day is today?
  What day is tomorrow?
  What day was yesterday?
  What did you do yesterday?
  What are you going to do tomorrow?
  Which days are weekdays?
  Which days are weekends?
  Which days do you come to school?

IN THE TEXT

- To introduce the vocabulary, see the suggested procedures in **TO THE TEACHER**.

Write

OBJECTIVE: To learn what a weekly schedule is and how to keep track of plans using a schedule.

- Explain what a weekly schedule is.
- Either fill out the weekly schedule on the transparency, or, on the board, draw one similar to the illustration in the text. Fill out the schedule.
- Tell the class about your weekly schedule as you are filling it out.
- Have students fill out their weekly schedules individually in their texts.
- Divide the class into pairs when they have completed their schedules.
- Have pairs tell each other about their schedules.
- Have individual students come to the board or transparency and fill in one of the boxes, then explain the box he or she filled out.
- Discuss the activities. Draw conclusions. For example, *Isn't this interesting! Many people go to the movies on Saturday evening.*
- Review any new vocabulary and write it on the board. Have students copy the new words into the **Vocabulary** section of their notebooks.

Partner Interview

- Follow the suggested procedures on page T4.

Group Survey

- Follow the suggested procedures on page T19.

EXPANSION

- Ask students what their favorite day of the week is. Why is it their favorite?
- Write the reasons on the board.

MONTHS AND DATES

WARM UP

- Bring in several different types of calendars to use in this unit. Have enough to distribute to groups of five or six. Try to get calendars with spaces for students to write in.
- Use a large wall calendar and an analog clock.
- As a review, ask what time it is. *When does class begin? Are we early for class? Are we late?*
- Ask what day it is. *What day is today? What day was yesterday?*
- Ask what month it is. *What month are we in? What was last month? What is next month going to be?*
- Ask if students like this month and why.
- Ask what happens in this month—holidays? birthdays? days off from school?
- Ask about the date. *What's today's date? Yesterday? Tomorrow?*
- Ask what year it is.
- Ask about the century. *What century is it now? What is the next century going to be?*

IN THE TEXT

- Look at the yearly calendar with the students, or show the transparency with books closed.
- To introduce the vocabulary, see the suggested procedures in **TO THE TEACHER.**
- Talk about dates (ordinal numbers) as you model the vocabulary on the text page. You may want to clarify the difference between **cardinal** numbers (numbers used in counting) and **ordinal** numbers.

Class Discussion
OBJECTIVE: To integrate new vocabulary into the context of students' experiences; to listen to other students' experiences and take notes.

- Ask the questions and call on different students for the answers.
- Try to involve as many students as possible in the discussion. Conduct this activity like a chain.
- Ask the first question; the first student answers it and asks Question 2 to the next (or a random) student, who answers it and asks Question 3.
- Continue around the room.
- If students can add more questions, have them dictate them as you write them on the board. Include these questions in the chain.
- Have students write new words and phrases in the **Vocabulary** section of their notebooks.

Group Activity
OBJECTIVE: To discuss significant dates and note them on a calendar.

- Divide the class into groups of five or six.
- To each group distribute one of the calendars you brought in.
- Explain that they are going to discuss important dates, such as birthdays, anniversaries, name days, and holidays.
- Have them brainstorm dates and write them either on their calendars in their text or on the calendars you provide.
- Have each group select a *recorder* to write down the dates on the calendars.
- Circulate around the room; help as needed.
- When students have completed their calendars, compare results. Start with January. Write JANUARY on the board and list all the important dates each group's recorder dictates.
- *Variation:* Draw a 12-month calendar with spaces to write what students will dictate. Either use the board or the transparency.

Class Game: *"What is your favorite month?"*

- Follow the suggested procedures for **Class Game** on page T5.

EXPANSION

- Have students write the months as you dictate them in random order.
- •• Talk about different types of calendars. Students' native countries may have different years (for example, the Asian and Hebrew calendars). If students can bring in calendars from their native countries, have them do so and explain them to the class.
- ••• Write the following sentence on the board: **There are** _____ _____ **in a** _____.
- Ask students to fill in the blanks. (There are *seven* days in a week; *thirty* or *thirty-one* days in a month; *twelve* months in a year; *one hundred* years in a century; *twenty-four* hours in a day.)
- *Variation:* Do this activity as a class or in groups. Whoever finishes first is the winner!

BIRTHDAYS

WARM UP

- Bring in supplies for birthday or name day celebrations, such as birthday cards, candles, party hats, signs that say, "Happy Birthday," etc.
- Arrange all the realia on a desk or table.
- Ask the class what these things are for. See how much they know.
- Invite individual students to pick an item and tell what it is and what it is for.
- Write new words on the board.
- Ask who is having a birthday soon. When is it? How is the student going to celebrate the birthday?
- Who just had a birthday? How did the student celebrate?

IN THE TEXT

- Let students take some time to absorb the scope of the picture.
- To introduce the vocabulary, see the suggested procedures in **TO THE TEACHER**.
- Talk to the students about the illustration. What is happening? Use the vocabulary.
- Point to the vocabulary item as you use the word.
- *Variation:* Have students tell *you* the story. Help by pointing out the items as students use the words.

What's the Story?

- Follow the suggested procedures on page T23, but divide into groups of four rather than three.

Partner Interview

- Follow the suggested procedures on page T4.

Write

OBJECTIVE: To learn to write simple greetings; to learn appropriate ways to sign a birthday card.

- Before students do this activity, use the birthday cards you brought in for the **WARM UP.** Talk about the custom of sending birthday cards.
- Tell students that people often write messages on the card as well as sign the card. Ask what kind of messages they think are appropriate. Write some on the board.
- Talk about different kinds of cards—funny, insulting, romantic, cards to different family members, etc.
- Ask what kind of card the one in the text is.
- Have partners do the activity together. When students have completed the activity, compare messages and information.
- Talk about the messages the students wrote and how they signed the cards.
- Ask how many students have birthdays in each month. Does anyone have the same birthday?

Cross-Cultural Exchange

OBJECTIVE: To exchange information about students' cultures and traditions regarding birthdays.

- Ask the questions and have students explain their customs.
- How many different languages are represented in the class? Have students write their language translation of *Happy Birthday* on the board and teach the pronunciation to the class.

EXPANSION

- Write the word B I R T H D A Y on the board. Either break students into groups of three or four, or work as a class to create a crossword puzzle.
- Have students attach any words they know to the word.
- If students work in groups, give them a set time to work in (for example, five minutes). The group with the most words is the winner!

EXAMPLE:

```
B I R T H D A Y
      E
      S E V E N
      T     I
      E     G
      R     H
      D     T I M E
      A
      Y E A R
```

HOLIDAYS

WARM UP

- Bring in holiday music and see if students can identify the holiday from the music (such as "Auld Lang Syne," Christmas carols, "The Star Spangled Banner," a love song).
- *Variation:* Use your picture file. Show illustrations of the different holidays and have students identify the holiday. Write appropriate vocabulary on the board.

IN THE TEXT

- With the students, look at the individual illustrations of the holidays on both pages, or show the transparency (frame by frame) with books closed.
- Talk about each holiday separately. Give the date and the name of the holiday.
- *Variation:* Ask students questions about the holidays and have them supply the information. (Yes/no questions are the easiest. For example, point to the illustration of New Year's Eve and ask *Is this Christmas? Are the people waiting for Santa Claus?* Have students supply the correct information.)
- Write the names of the holidays and the dates on the board.
- Also write the corresponding vocabulary for each holiday on the board.
- Have students discuss the holidays. (Do they celebrate each one? How do they celebrate? What do they know about the origins of each holiday, etc.) Are there similar holidays in their countries? (For example, when is Independence Day? How is it celebrated?)

Class Activity

OBJECTIVE: To discuss holidays.

- Have students write the dates of the holidays celebrated in the United States under each illustration.
- Ask different students what their favorite holiday is and why.
- Take advantage of any cross-cultural information that springs from this activity.
- Write any new vocabulary on the board. Have students copy the words into the **Vocabulary** section of their notebooks.

Conversation Squares

OBJECTIVE: To interview classmates about favorite holidays.

- Have the students help you create the questions they will need for each square.
- Write the questions on the board.
- Construct boxes on the board similar to the ones in the text.
- Choose two students. Use yourself as the third member of the group.
- Put the three names on the top of the boxes as indicated in the text.
- Ask and answer the questions for your box; write in your responses.
- Ask your "partners" the questions. Write their responses.
- Then ask the class the questions for more practice.
- Have groups of three do the activity.
- When all students have finished, ask different groups single questions from the conversation squares. Review any new vocabulary and write it on the board.
- Have students copy the new words into the **Vocabulary** section of their notebooks.

Cross-Cultural Exchange

OBJECTIVE: To exchange information about students' cultures and traditions regarding holidays.

- Ask students how to say "Merry Christmas" and "Happy New Year" in their native languages. Have them write their language translation on the board and teach the pronunciation to the class.
- Have students teach the class other holiday greetings from their countries.

Speech

OBJECTIVE: To reinforce important holiday vocabulary by using it in a formal presentation to the class.

- Read the instructions aloud. Model a very brief speech.
- Make copies of the **Speech** and **Audience Evaluation** forms in the **student text APPENDIX**, page 248.
- Have students prepare speeches at home. The speech should be between one and two minutes long.
- Help students correct their speeches.
- Have the students prepare notecards so they won't be reading their speeches to the class.
- Assign different students to be *evaluators* for each speaker.
- Collect their evaluations at the end of the class. Review the evaluations, add comments, and return them to the speakers.
- Remember to applaud all the speeches!

EXPANSION

- Depending on what month you teach this unit, feature the holiday for the month. Bring in realia relating to the holiday.
- Discuss with the class the significance of the realia. Ask the class about similar holidays in their countries and about celebrations and acknowledgments of the holidays.

SEASONS

WARM UP

- Depending upon the season in which you are teaching this lesson, bring in items or pictures appropriate for that season. (For example, if it is winter, bring in Christmas wrapping paper, Christmas greeting cards, Chanukah items, clothing and other items for the appropriate weather conditions.)
- Pantomime actions for each item. Ask the students what you are doing.
- Ask what season it is.
- Do the same for other seasons. Have students do some of the pantomiming. No one should speak except the student who guesses the season.
- Ask students what they do in each season.
- Gear the discussion to your geography and the appropriate season.
- *Variation:* Use illustrations of different seasons from your picture file. Either describe the season and what the people are doing in the illustrations or ask students yes/no questions about what is happening. You can vary this activity by giving a more knowledgeable student an illustration and have that student ask the yes/no questions.

IN THE TEXT

- Look at the illustrations with the students or show the transparency with books closed.
- Let students take some time to absorb the scope of the illustrations.
- To introduce the vocabulary, see the suggested procedures in **TO THE TEACHER**.
- *Variation:* Show one frame at a time, rather than the entire illustration.
- Have students describe each scene; supply vocabulary where needed. Write the new words on the board for students to copy into their texts or into the **Vocabulary** section of their notebooks.

Class Discussion

OBJECTIVE: To integrate new vocabulary into the context of students' experiences; to listen to other students' experiences and take notes.

- Ask the questions and call on different students for the answers.
- Try to involve as many students as possible in the discussion.
- Write new vocabulary on the board as it comes up in conversation.
- Have students copy the new words into the **Vocabulary** section of their notebooks.
- (If there are students from climates where the seasons are very different, use the information to draw conclusions and teach students about different seasons in the world according to geographical location.)
- To help structure discussions and teach note-taking skills, write a brief heading for each question on the board. Encourage students to do the same in the **Activities** section of their notebooks. Under each heading list information you gather from the discussions. Then review your notes and ask the students to review theirs. Draw conclusions together from the notes at the end of the discussion.

What's the Story?

- Follow the suggested procedures on page T23.

Partner Game: *"What do you remember?"*

OBJECTIVE: To test observation and practice remembering detail.

- Divide the class into pairs.
- Partners are going to look at the illustration and discuss it. Talk about ways for the students to remember the details of the illustration. Then have students close their texts.
- Have partners list everything they can remember together about the illustration.
- Pair partner groups so there are groups of four. Have the groups compare notes and amend their lists.
- Have groups report what they remember about the illustration to the class.
- Give each group a letter name. On the board, write the number of details each group had next to the letter. (For example, if group A had eight items, write A–8; if B had six, write B–6 below the A–8, etc.)
- Have students open their texts to page 35 or show the transparency of the illustration.
- Have students compare their notes with the illustration.
- Which group of four had the most correct detail? They are the winners!

EXPANSION

- Divide the class into four groups. Either assign a season or let students choose one. Each group must represent a different season.
- Have students discuss and list the activities that they would recommend for "their" season. Each group should have a *recorder*.
- Give students a specific time frame, perhaps ten minutes. Give a one-minute warning at nine minutes. Then, at ten minutes, say *Time's up!*
- Have each recorder make recommendations to the class as to what activities to do in his or her season. Write new words on the board for the class to copy into the **Vocabulary** section of their notebooks.

WEATHER

WARM UP

- Use your picture file. Either show the entire class an illustration, or give groups or individual students each an illustration depicting weather and seasons. Tell students about the illustration you are holding up, or have students talk about their illustration.
- Emphasize the weather conditions in each, but review seasons as much as possible.
- Ask what month and date students think the illustration shows.

IN THE TEXT

- Look at the illustrations on both pages with the students or show the transparency with books closed.
- *Variation:* Show one frame at a time rather than the entire illustration.
- To introduce the vocabulary, see the suggested procedures in **TO THE TEACHER**.

Class Discussion

OBJECTIVE: To use new vocabulary to describe each weather scene.

- Show the frames individually. Ask the class to talk about each frame.
- Have the class be imaginative and tell you about the people in the illustrations. (For example, *What are their names? What is their relationship? Where are they from? What day of the week is it? What is the date? Where are they? What is happening? What are they going to do?*)
- With the class, tell the story of each scene.
- *Variation:* Break the students into small groups or into pairs to write the story, and have them tell their story to the class. Having pairs will lead more easily into the next activity.

Partner Interview

- Follow the suggested procedures on page T4.

Find Someone Who

- Follow the suggested procedures on page T12.

EXPANSION

- Do a modified TPR–type activity as the one illustrated on **student text** page 5.
- Also note the explanation on page T17. (**What am I doing?**)
- Give out a slip of paper to each student.
- Tell them to think of a weather condition (**hot, sunny, rainy,** etc.).
- Write a weather condition on your paper. Have students write a weather condition on their paper.
- Fold your paper. Have students fold their papers.
- Start a pile of papers with your folded paper. Have students come up and put their folded papers on top of yours. Shuffle the pile of papers.
- Open the first one. DON'T read it—act it out.
- Whoever guesses the weather condition comes up and picks the next paper, acts the condition out, and waits for a student to guess.
- The student who guesses picks the next paper.

WEATHER REPORT

WARM UP

- If you have access to a television or a VCR, watch a weather report with the class.
- Talk about today's weather and the report. *Who is giving the report? Is the report for the whole country or only a local section? What is the report? How accurate is the report? What can you expect for weather in the next few days?* etc.
- Bring in weather maps from newspapers. The weather map in *USA TODAY* is a good one to use.
- Distribute enough copies for students to look at. Ask questions such as *What's the weather like in _____? Where is it raining?*
- Encourage students to bring in weather maps from their native language newspapers. (Use in **Community Activities** below.)

IN THE TEXT

- Look at the illustration with the students or show the transparency with books closed.
- To introduce the vocabulary, see the suggested procedures in **TO THE TEACHER**.

Group Activity

OBJECTIVE: To integrate new vocabulary into the context of students' experiences; to listen to other students' experiences and take notes.

- Divide students into groups of three.
- Refer to the map in the **student text APPENDIX**, page 244, and discuss which states constitute the different sections of the country.
- Have the groups look at the illustration and divide the map into the five sections.
- Then have them make up a weather forecast for each of the areas.
- Each student in each group should have a different area.
- Have each group explain their forecasts to another group.

Community Activities

OBJECTIVE: To relate vocabulary and structures to "real-life" weather reports.

- Have the class use the native language weather reports they brought in from home (see **WARM UP**).
- Have students report on the weather in their countries or cities.
- Discuss how weather forecasts differ in newspapers from different regions.

- •• Have students watch a weather report on TV—in English, if possible.
- Have them take notes and report on their findings the next day.
- Who watched the same channel? Which report was the most accurate? Why?

EXPANSION

- "20 Questions" Game: Have one student think of a place. Have the class ask 20 questions about the weather to guess the place.
- Have partners role play a weather forecast.

SEASONAL CLOTHING

WARM UP

- Bring in typical clothing for different seasons. Don't limit yourself to the words on the list.
- Call on individual students to put on one item of clothing. Ask what weather the item is for. (For example, if a student puts on a ski hat or goggles, students guess *winter* or *summer* depending on the hemisphere!)
- This activity presents a good opportunity to review clothing, colors, and pairs from Unit 1, pages 8–9.
- *Variation:* Use illustrations from your picture file for this activity.

IN THE TEXT

- Look at the illustration with the students or show the transparency with books closed.
- As you point to each separate article, ask students to name the articles of clothing they know.
- To introduce the vocabulary, see the suggested procedures in **TO THE TEACHER**.

Partner Interview

- Follow the suggested procedures on page T4.

Speech

OBJECTIVE: To reinforce important weather vocabulary by using it in a formal presentation to the class; to share personal experiences.

- Read the instructions aloud. Add other questions with the class.
- Have students prepare at home a short speech about the weather in their hometown. The speech should be between three and four minutes.
- Help students correct their speeches. Have students prepare notecards so they won't be *reading* the speech to the class.
- Have students practice the speech either with you or in groups of four or five.
- Make copies of the **Speech** and **Audience Evaluation** forms in the **student text APPENDIX**, page 248.
- Assign different students to be *evaluators* for each speaker.
- Collect their evaluations at the end of the class. Review the evaluations, add comments, and return them to the speakers.
- Remember to applaud all speeches.
- Discuss the evaluations in the next class if appropriate. Keep the comments positive!

EXPANSION

- Do a chain activity. Start by saying *It's cold. **What do I wear?***
- Ask the first student in the row or circle. That student answers and makes a similar statement, such as *It's snowing. **What do I do?*** The next student answers and asks the next question.
- You can do this as a chain or have students choose random students to answer and ask.

REVIEW

IN THE TEXT

Partner Interview

- Follow the suggested procedures on page T4.

Write

OBJECTIVE: To practice writing information about weather; to transfer oral information to written form.

- Have students do their individual journal writing.
- Circulate; help as needed.

Tell Your Partner

OBJECTIVE: To read, listen, and talk about written expression.

- Have students read their journal entries to their partners.
- Have several students read their journal entries to the class.
- Follow the instructions on page T7, **Tell the Class** for writing some journals on the board.

EXPANSION

- Bring in a "Calendar Grab Bag." Fill it with assorted items relevant to this unit, such as a calendar (either a day or month calendar), items from different seasons, seasonal clothing, a weather report, items for a birthday party, etc.
- *Variation:* Have students bring in one item associated with any page of this unit. Put the items in a large bag or box.
- Either do this activity as a class or in large groups. (For groups, you will need one bag or box per group.)
- Have individual students select an item and identify it.
- *Variation:* The student who chooses the item asks a question, such as **When do you wear a party hat?** Whoever answers chooses the next item.
- If possible, have students categorize the items. Write columns on the board, such as CALENDAR, SEASONAL, BIRTHDAYS, etc. As students select items, have them tell you where to categorize that item.

- •• Review all illustrations in the unit or show the transparencies from Unit 3 again.
- Have students make up questions about the illustrations. Write their questions on the board. Have individual students choose a question and ask either a specific student or anyone in the class. When that student answers, he or she asks the next question.

UNIT TEST

- A **conversation test** and a **vocabulary test** for this unit are located in the back of this Teacher's Guide, plus suggestions for administration. Feel free to make as many copies as you need.

NET. WT. 1.25 oz.

CARVER ❀ FOTINOS

FOOD

LEARNING STRATEGIES

➤ Have lunch with one or more friends. Speak only English at lunch.

➤ Find food labels in English. Read the labels out loud. Ask your teacher about the pronunciation of new words.

FRUIT

WARM UP

- Bring as many real fruits to class as possible.
- Arrange the fruit on a table.
- On individual index cards, write the words of the different fruits that you brought to class.
- Give each student a card with the name of a fruit. Have students match the card and the fruit on the table. Have the students leave the card next to the fruit.
- List the vocabulary for the fruits on the board. Ask students the words in their native languages. (Students should come to the board and write their word next to the English word.)
- Have students add to the list any other fruits they know. If they only know the word in their language, have them write that. You can fill in the English later.

IN THE TEXT

- Look at the illustration with the students or show the transparency with books closed.
- Ask about the illustration: *Where are the people? Who is there? What are they doing?*
- To introduce the vocabulary, see the suggested procedures in **TO THE TEACHER**.
- Ask students to describe different fruits in the picture. For example, have them tell the *color*, the *size*, whether it has a *pit* or *seeds*, whether you have to *peel* it or not and how it is sold (e.g., *by the pound, box, bunch, individually,* etc.).

Partner Interview

- Follow the suggested procedures on page T4.

Group Game: *"Preparing fruit salad"*

OBJECTIVE: To work cooperatively in a group to plan and carry out the task of preparing a fruit salad; to explain the process to the class.

- Explain to students that they will be preparing fruit salad in the next class.
- Divide the class into groups of four and assign each group a number.
- In their groups, students should decide what to bring. Each student should be responsible for at least one item (bowl, knife, large spoon, napkins, paper plates, spoons or forks for the group, and different fruits).
- Each student should make a list of what he or she is responsible for.
- Bring "back up" supplies: knives, peelers, plastic utensils, paper plates or bowls, and napkins.
- In the next class, have each group meet to rehearse. Each group will prepare their salad in front of the class.
- Group 1 should prepare their salad in front of the class and explain what they are doing. Write the steps on the board.
- Repeat this procedure with all groups.
- Line up all the salads on a table. Put a card in front of each with the group's number.
- Have the class vote on the best fruit salad.
- Have one student from each group serve his/her group's fruit salad to the class.

EXPANSION

- Have the class dictate the vocabulary for different fruits they like.
- Write the fruits on the board in a vertical list.
- Point to each fruit and say it. Then say *Raise your hand if your favorite fruit is _____.*
- Count hands. Have the class decide on their most popular fruit. Ask why people like their fruit.

- •• Set the scene. *You are in a fruit market and want to buy some fruit.*
- Explain that students will take roles and write a conversation between the vendor (clerk) and the customer.
- If necessary, write a sample role play on the board together with the class. Since this is the first time students will be writing a role play, be very sure they understand what to do.
- Divide the class into pairs.
- Give students time to complete their role play and to practice it.
- Circulate; help as needed.
- Have several pairs present their role play to the class.
- Write new vocabulary on the board. Have students copy the new vocabulary into the **Vocabulary** section of their notebooks.

- ••• Play "20 Questions." Start by saying *I'm thinking of a fruit. It's red.*
- Have students ask yes/no questions until a student guesses.
- That student gets to be the leader next.

- •••• Have students bring their favorite fruit to class and tell the class about it.

VEGETABLES

WARM UP

- From local supermarkets, bring in enough circulars for every student in the class. Keep these for use during the entire unit of **FOOD**.
- Ask students which vegetables are advertised in the circular. Which do they recognize? Which do they buy? Where do they buy their vegetables?
- Ask students if they ever look at these circulars. Do they buy items according to sales? Which items are the best buys this week?
- On the board, list the vegetables the students name as they call them out.
- Ask if any students can add vegetables not listed in the circulars.
- Have students come to the board and write their native language equivalent next to each vegetable.

IN THE TEXT

- Look at the illustration with the students or show the transparency with books closed.
- Talk about the illustration. Have students help you tell a story about it.
- To introduce the vocabulary, see the suggested procedures in **TO THE TEACHER**.
- Be sure to explain the words *head* (of lettuce) and *ear* (of corn).

Partner Interview

- Follow the suggested procedures on page T4.

Group Decision

OBJECTIVE: To discuss and decide as a group how to complete the task of making a salad.

- Divide the students into groups of five or six.
- Review the instructions with the class.
- You may want to prepare for this activity by using *carrots* as an example for the vocabulary. Have a pot, a parer, a shredder, and a knife.
- Demonstrate the vocabulary to the students. For example, peel the carrot and ask what you are doing. When students say *peeling the carrot* put the vocabulary on the board. Continue with all words.
- Tell each group to decide together which vegetables to use and how to prepare each one to make a salad.
- Circulate; help as needed.
- Have a *reporter* from each group tell the class about the group's salad.
- Compare decisions.

EXPANSION

- Ask students to bring in other market circulars and newspaper ads. Collect their circulars for use later in this unit.

- •• Play "Concentration." Prepare a board with names and pictures of ten vegetables in random order. Each vegetable should be represented twice: once by a picture and once by the word for the vegetable.
- Put paper slips over all the words and pictures.
- Have students divide into two teams. One team starts and says the name of a vegetable. That team tries to find the match. If they succeed, reveal both the illustration and the word. The same team then has another turn. If they don't get a match, the other team has a turn.
- Continue until all the words and pictures are revealed. Which team got the most matches?

- ••• Make vegetable soup. Have the class brainstorm what to put into the pot.
- List the ingredients on the board. Write a recipe.
- If possible, prepare the soup in school.
- Ask about different recipes for vegetable soup.

- •••• Do students drink vegetable juices? What kinds? List them on the board.

MEAT, SEAFOOD, AND POULTRY

WARM UP

- Use the supermarket circulars from the previous pages. Pass them out to all students.
- Ask students which meats, seafood, and poultry are advertised. Explain the categories of meat, seafood, and poultry.
- Have students compare their circulars to the items in their books or on the transparency.
- Which items are students familiar with? Which do they buy?
- Which items do people eat in their countries? How are they prepared?
- Do students ever eat *raw* meat? *raw* fish? How is it prepared?

IN THE TEXT

- To introduce the vocabulary, see the suggested procedures in **TO THE TEACHER**.
- Talk about the illustration. *Where is it taking place? Who are the people? What are they doing? What are they going to do with the items they buy? What else are they going to buy in the supermarket?*
- Which words were used? Which are new vocabulary words? (Be sure students know what *poultry* is!)

Partner Interview

- Follow the suggested procedures on page T4.

IN THE TEXT

- Bring in illustrations from your illustration file, or from cookbooks, magazines, or other sources that show food being prepared or cooked.
- Ask students how they prepare different meats, seafood, and poultry.
- To introduce the vocabulary, see the suggested procedures in **TO THE TEACHER**.
- Explain each preparation. Ask students if they like their food prepared this way.
- Ask students about other ways to prepare the foods discussed.

Find Someone Who

OBJECTIVE: To ask yes/no questions; to share personal information with classmates.

- Be sure students know the vocabulary as well as how to structure their questions. *(Do you like, eat, prepare, broil _____? Do you know how to _____?)*
- Have students circulate in the class or in a large group (10 to 15) to get answers. As they complete the questions, they should return to their seats.
- Who finished first?
- When all students have completed their work, go over the questions. Draw conclusions about the likes and dislikes and eating customs of the class.
- Use the opportunity to expand on any interesting topics that arise during the activity.

EXPANSION

- Brainstorm with the students a list of their favorite main dishes.
- •• Ask students to explain a meal to the class or to smaller groups.
- ••• Have a pot luck dinner or lunch with dishes the students bring to class.

DESSERTS

WARM UP

- Begin class with a coffee and dessert party!
- Have different coffees—Turkish, Colombian, Arabic, African—and different types of teas.
- Bring in different desserts or have students bring in desserts.
- Have students talk about the desserts and coffees and teas.
- Exchange ideas about different cultures' desserts and beverages.

IN THE TEXT

- To introduce the vocabulary, see the suggested procedures in **TO THE TEACHER**.
- Talk about the scene. Have students help you talk about the scene. Ask:

  What is happening in the picture?
  What items can you identify?
  What are the people's names?
  What are they doing?
  What time is it?
  What would you choose to have for dessert at this place?
  Where would you like to sit?

What's the Story?

- Follow the suggested procedures on page T23, but divide into groups of five rather than three.

Group Discussion

OBJECTIVE: To integrate new vocabulary into the context of students' experiences; to listen to other students' experiences and take notes; to practice including others in a discussion.

- Divide the class into groups of five.
- Have each group decide upon a *leader* and a *recorder* to take notes.
- Have the leader ask the questions; have the recorder take notes and report back to the class on the group's conclusions when all groups have completed the activity.
- How many different desserts were mentioned?
- What conclusions did students arrive at regarding fattening desserts (question 4)?
- What do students think about desserts—do they like them? Do they eat them? Do they buy them or prepare them?

Group Role Play

OBJECTIVE: To create a story and role play it with a group.

- Have students stay in their same groups.
- Be sure students understand the instructions.
- In their groups, have them decide on how to fill in the dessert menu. Circulate; help as needed.
- Have students write a short role play at a coffee shop. Each student should have a role. (Possible roles: waiter or waitress, customers, cashier, etc.)
- Have several groups present their role plays to the class.
- Write polite phrases on the board for students to copy into the **Vocabulary** section of their notebooks. (***Are you ready to order? I'd like _____***, etc.)
- Discuss restaurant etiquette and customs in different cultures.

Cross-Cultural Exchange

OBJECTIVE: To exchange information about desserts.

- If you did not do so at the beginning of this lesson, have the class bring their favorite desserts to class.
- Have each student explain what the dessert is and why he or she likes it.
- Arrange the desserts on a table. Write the name of each dessert on a card in front of it.
- Have a tasting party! Which dessert is the class' favorite?

EXPANSION

- Play a version of "Jeopardy!" Write individual cards for different desserts on the word list. Have two bells or noisemakers.
- Make a pile of the cards.
- Divide the class into two teams. Give each team a bell or noisemaker; tell the students to ring the bells when they have the correct answer.
- Tell the class you will read the name of a dessert. Tell the teams to think of a question whose answer is the word you said. For example, you read ***brownie.***
- The teams must come up with a question such as ***What is a soft brown square chocolate cookie with nuts?*** and ring their bells when they are ready.
- The team that gives the first correct *question* gets a point.
- Continue the game until you have used all the cards. Which team won?

BREAKFAST

WARM UP

- Use your picture file or illustrations from magazines of real breakfast foods (or just the cartons and wrappers).
- Have students identify items from the illustrations. Write the words on the board.
- Bring cereal boxes, orange juice cartons, coffee cans, tea boxes, etc., to class. Have individual students or groups make groupings of their favorite breakfasts with these items.
- Have students explain their breakfasts. What do they like that isn't on the table?

IN THE TEXT

- To introduce the vocabulary, see the suggested procedures in **TO THE TEACHER.**
- Talk about what is happening in the picture: *What time is it? What are the people's names? What are the children eating? the adults? What is the family talking about? Is the father happy that the girl is petting the dog? Why? Why not?*
- *Variation:* Have students tell you the questions they want to ask. Write the questions on the board. When you have brainstormed the questions, ask the class the answers.
- Ask such questions as:

  What time do you eat breakfast?
  Who do you eat with?
  What is your typical breakfast during the week? on the weekend?

Partner Interview

- Follow the suggested procedures on page T4.

Cross-Cultural Exchange

OBJECTIVE: To exchange information about breakfast foods in students' countries.

- Ask the questions and have students explain their customs for breakfast.
- Discuss different breakfast habits. *Where do students eat breakfast? What time do they have breakfast?* etc.
- Have students bring in any foods they can and have the class sample them.

Conversation Squares

OBJECTIVE: To interview classmates about common breakfast foods in different countries.

- Follow the suggested procedures on page T33.

Group Survey

- Follow the suggested procedures on page T19.
- Point out adverbs of frequency with *how often* questions.
- When all the groups complete their work, go over the questions. Draw conclusions about the likes, dislikes, and breakfast customs of the class.
- Use the opportunity to expand on any interesting topics that arise during the activity.

EXPANSION

- With the class, write a conversation for the family's breakfast.
- Assign roles. Have students role play the conversation.
- Use phrases such as *Please pass the _____. Would you like some _____? Is there any _____? What are your plans for _____? Please don't feed the dog at the table.*

- •• Do a *word association* game. Write EGG on the board. Ask *What words do you think of when you see the word EGG?* Elicit some or all of the following words from the students.

ham	scrambled
hard boiled	fried
poached	sunny side up

- Write BREAKFAST on the board. Ask *What words do you think of when you see the word BREAKFAST?* Elicit some or all of the following words from the students.

toast	cereal
juice	healthy
cocoa	bacon
French toast	

- ••• Have students in groups role play having breakfast in a restaurant.

- •••• Discuss students' concepts of the American breakfast. Which do they prefer—their breakfasts or American-style breakfasts?

LUNCH

WARM UP

- If you can, gather simple lunch menus or circulars from neighborhood restaurants and coffee shops. If you can't get a variety, use only one and make copies.
- Give each student a menu. Ask *What do you want for lunch today (or tomorrow)?*
- Have the students individually select a lunch they would like to have.
- Call on several students to tell the class what they would like to have for lunch.
- List new words on the board.
- Follow up by asking what students usually have, what they had yesterday, if they have different lunches on weekends and weekdays, and so on.

IN THE TEXT

- To introduce the vocabulary, see the suggested procedures in **TO THE TEACHER.**
- Ask if anyone has a *microwave oven*. When do they use it?
- Ask if anyone buys *frozen foods*. Divide the class into groups of five or six and have the groups brainstorm a list of the things they buy in the frozen food section. Combine lists on the board.
- Ask students if they ever have *leftovers*. What do they do with leftovers? Do they eat them for lunch the next day?
- Ask if people eat frozen foods in their countries. Which ones? What do people freeze in their homes?

What's the Story?

- Follow the suggested procedures on page T23, but divide into groups of five rather than three.

Partner Interview

- Follow the suggested procedures on page T4.

Write

OBJECTIVE: To express preference for a sandwich type and explain how to prepare it.

- Before students write their recipes, ask them about their favorite sandwiches. On the board make a list of favorite sandwiches.
- Review the vocabulary. Be sure students understand all the words.
- Ask students how to prepare their favorite sandwich. On the board, draw a replica of the notebook paper on page 53. Write one of the student's recipes on the board.
- Have the student whose recipe you wrote read the recipe. Then erase the fill-ins, but leave the skeleton.
- Have students individually write recipes for their favorite sandwiches in their texts. Circulate; help as needed.
- Have several students read their recipes for favorite sandwiches.
- *Variation:* Have students come to the board and fill in the blanks on the replica.
- As a follow up, ask what students like to eat with their sandwich: *soup? chips? salad?* What do they like to drink with their sandwich: *milk? juice? coffee?*

EXPANSION

- Ask students if they ever have soup for lunch. What kind? List students' favorites on the board.
- Ask students what kinds of soups people eat in their countries. What are the ingredients?
- Does anyone have soup when they are sick? *What kinds of soup are best when you are sick?*

•• Have students bring in their favorite recipes for anything. Make a recipe book of the class' favorite recipes.

••• Discuss lunch customs around the world. Ask questions such as:

What time do people eat lunch in your country?
Do people usually eat lunch at home?
Do people sometimes eat lunch in restaurants?
Do many people eat lunch at work? At school?
Do people take naps during lunch time?
How is lunch different on the weekend and during the week?

•••• What do students think of lunch habits in the United States and Canada?

FAST FOOD

WARM UP

- Ask the class if they know any fast-food restaurants near the school.
- List them horizontally.
- Ask *What are the specialties in each fast-food restaurant?*
- List the foods under each heading.
- Ask *Who has eaten at each of these restaurants? What have you ordered? When did you eat there last? Was the food good? Was the service good?*
- If there are no fast-food restaurants in the school neighborhood, gear the questions to the students' neighborhood.

IN THE TEXT

- To introduce the vocabulary, see the suggested procedures in **TO THE TEACHER**.
- Ask students if they ever use the *Take Out* or *Drive Thru* at fast-food restaurants. Do they ever use the *salad bar*? What do they get in their salads?
- What is a *hamburger with the works*?
- Are there fast-food restaurants in the students' countries? Which ones? Do people like to eat there? Is the food the same as in the United States?

Group Survey

- Follow the suggested procedures on page T19.
- What do students like most? What do they like least? Do they think fast foods are bad to eat?

Partner Role Play

OBJECTIVE: To write and perform a role play in which to review new vocabulary and structures in a given context.

- Set the scene. Have students pretend they are in a fast-food restaurant.
- Explain that students will take roles and write a conversation between the cashier and a customer.
- This role play is a partial dialog. Read the partial dialogs to the students. Explain what kinds of phrases are needed to fit into the missing parts. Have the students make suggestions.
- If necessary, write a sample role play on the board together with the class.
- Give students time to complete their role-play conversation and practice it.
- Circulate; help as needed.
- Have several students present their role plays to the class.
- Write new vocabulary on the board. Have students copy the new vocabulary into the **Vocabulary** section of their notebooks.

EXPANSION

- Change the role play. Tell the students the customer gives the cashier $20 and gets too much change. Ask students to write an appropriate ending to the role play when the customer realizes there was an error.
- Discuss with students what to do if they are given the wrong change in a store or restaurant.

- •• Change the role play again. Have students role play asking for change. Have students and their partners decide what they need change for (a pay phone, the bus, a soda machine, etc.), who they are asking for the change (a friend, a salesclerk, a passerby, etc.), and how much money they need to ask for (a $5 bill, for example).

JUNK FOOD

WARM UP

- Bring in some of the junk food listed in the vocabulary box and/or other examples of junk food.
- *Variation:* Ask students to bring in samples of their favorite snacks.
- Arrange the junk food on a desk or table. Ask individual students to come up and choose their favorite. Why do they like it?
- How many students eat junk food? Who NEVER eats junk food?
- Ask **Why do you eat junk food?**
  When do you eat junk food
  Where do you buy junk food?
  What kinds of snacks are healthier than junk food? etc.
- If students have brought in sample snacks, have them show the class, and have the class decide if the snack is healthy or not.

IN THE TEXT

- How many of these snacks do the students know?
- Ask for brand names of these snacks. List the names on the board.
- Ask students if they use **vending machines**. Are there differences in vending machines in their countries and the United States?
- To introduce the vocabulary, see the suggested procedures in **TO THE TEACHER**.

Class Discussion

- Follow the suggested procedures on page T29.

Class Game: *"What is your favorite junk food?"*

- Follow the suggested procedures on page T5.

Group Decision

OBJECTIVE: To discuss the task with other students and to come to a group decision about how to spend five dollars.

- Divide students into groups of five or six.
- Explain that they will be making a group decision as to how to spend $5.00 on snacks. Have the groups choose a *reporter* who will report the decisions.
- Set a time limit of five to seven minutes. Have them decide as a group what they will buy.

EXPANSION

- In groups of three, create TV commercials for snacks. Videotape the commercials and play them for the class.

DINNER

WARM UP

- Ask *Do you ever "eat out"?*
  Where ?
  Who do you go with?
  What do you like to eat when you go out?
  What is your favorite restaurant?
- Make two lists on the board: EATING AT HOME and EATING OUT.
- Have students call out the food they like to eat at home and the food they like to eat in a restaurant. Have them tell you which column to write the food under.
- Ask *why?* questions. *Why do you like to eat certain foods at home? At a restaurant?*
- Tell students that you are having out-of-town guests and want to take them to the best restaurant in town. What is their recommendation? List the restaurants on the board. Ask why students gave you their selection.

IN THE TEXT

- To introduce the vocabulary, see the suggested procedures in **TO THE TEACHER.**
- Ask about the illustration. *Where are the people? What are they doing? What time is it?* etc.
- Ask a student to come to the front of the room. Have the student "play teacher" and point to objects in the illustration as the class says what they are.

What's the Story?

- Follow the suggested procedures on page T23, but divide into groups of five rather than three.

EXPANSION

- Discuss polite dinner table manners. Some possible topics: getting the attention of a waiter or waitress; who pays the bill (on a date, in a large group, with a family). Also ask about tipping, noise, smoking, etc.

- •• Ask about *foreign food* restaurants in students' countries. Which are most popular? What foreign foods do students like?

THE SUPERMARKET

WARM UP

- Use the same circulars you used at the beginning of the unit.
- Also bring in any supermarket coupons you have.
- Divide the class into groups of five or six.
- Distribute the circulars to each group—either one to a group, or one to each student in the group. The circulars must be the same within the group, but different groups can have different circulars.
- Have students decide what to buy for the week's groceries. Tell them to pay special attention to the specials, the sales, and the coupons. Have them estimate the cost of their week's shopping.
- Lay out the coupons on a table. Students can come up and take one to apply to their grocery list if they need it.
- Tell the groups to appoint a *recorder* to write down the grocery list and report back to the class.
- Set a time limit: 15 to 20 minutes.
- Have the recorders report back to the class. Other groups can ask questions such as *Why did you decide to buy eight dozen eggs? Why didn't you decide to buy any milk?*
- Anyone in the reporting group can answer the questions.

IN THE TEXT

- Ask students if they shop in a supermarket. Which one? Have the students look at the illustrations on both pages of the text, or show the transparency with books closed.
- To introduce the vocabulary, see the suggested procedures in **TO THE TEACHER.**

Group Vocabulary Challenge

- Follow the suggested procedures on page T17.

Group Decision

OBJECTIVE: To work as a group to complete the task of comparing prices.

- Divide students into groups of three or four.
- Talk about *comparison shopping*. Explain all the vocabulary and concepts. Be sure students understand that sometimes the larger the size, the *cheaper* per ounce it actually is, and the more *economical*.
- Have student groups check off answers on the tomato sauce chart. *Which is the largest jar? the smallest? the most expensive?* etc.
- While students are working, copy the chart and the art (jars, prices and weights of tomato sauce) on the board.
- Have students report their answers and explain why they made the decisions they did.

Community Activity

OBJECTIVE: To use the community as a resource to find information using the vocabulary and structures taught in class.

- Before sending students to the supermarket, review the task with them.
- Be sure they understand the vocabulary and the task.
- Explain that they must go to the supermarket with their books and take notes.
- Have them decide individually on the last two items they want to research.
- Explain how they should look for the size (weight or measure), the brand name, and the price. You might also ask them to note the unit price.
- If convenient and possible, take a class field trip to the supermarket. Inform the manager in advance of your arrival. Perhaps the class can get a tour of the back rooms!
- Have the students do their research and report back in the next class.
- Who found the best buys?
- What are the students' recommendations?

EXPANSION

- Play a supermarket chain game. Begin by saying *I'm going to the supermarket to buy an apple.* Student 1 has to repeat the sentence and add an item beginning with the last letter of the food item, in this case, *e: I'm going to the supermarket to buy an apple and an egg.* Student 2 repeats the sentence and adds a word beginning with *g: I'm going to buy an apple, an egg, and a grape.* Student 3 has to do the same and add a food or supermarket supply starting with *e.* Continue around the room.

- •• Have individual students make a shopping list of the things they usually buy.
- Compare lists. Who wrote the same things? What are they?
- Did anyone write a list in English? Who wrote a bilingual list?
- What foods from students' countries are on the lists?
- Who had the longest list? Who had the shortest list?
- Can the students estimate the cost of their lists?

REVIEW

IN THE TEXT

Group Decision

OBJECTIVE: To work as a group to complete the task of creating menus.

- Break students into groups of five or six.
- Tell students they are going to plan a day's menu for one of the groups of people in the illustration.
- Have them look at the illustrations and pick one group to plan a menu for.
- *Variation:* Assign each group a picture to ensure that all the pictures are described.
- Tell students to plan a food menu—breakfast, lunch, dinner, snacks—for one day.
- Have them list the family's menu for each meal and the cost for each meal.
- How much will the total cost be for the day's meals for the family?
- Have the groups report back to the class.
- Who spent the most per person? Who spent the least?

Class Game: *"What is it?"*

OBJECTIVE: To integrate vocabulary and ask yes/no questions about food.

- Students played this game in small groups on page 15 in the **student text**.
- You be the leader first. Say *I'm thinking of a food. You can eat it raw or cooked.*
- Students ask yes/no questions.
- When a student guesses the correct food, that student becomes the leader and the game continues. You are now part of the class.
- Review any new vocabulary and write it on the board. Have students copy the new words into the **Vocabulary** section of their notebooks.

Cross-Cultural Exchange

OBJECTIVE: To exchange information about students' cultures and experiences in a party setting.

- This is an opportunity for students to share their cultures with the class.
- Have everyone bring in a food common to their country and culture.
- Have students bring in their favorite typical music too.
- You can also have students write small index cards with the name of their dish and place it in front of the serving bowl or plate.

EXPANSION

- Ask students to compare typically American cuisine to their typical foods. For example, ask about sandwiches. Do students' cultures have anything similar (such as tortillas)?

UNIT TEST

- A **conversation test** and a **vocabulary test** for this unit are located in the back of this Teacher's Guide, plus suggestions for administration. Feel free to make as many copies as you need.

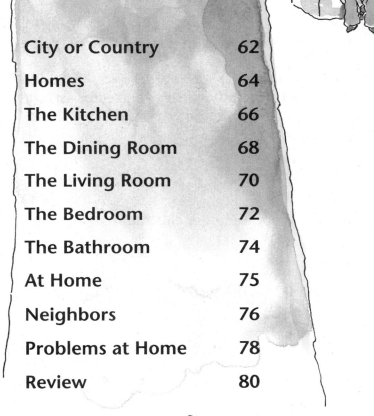

HOMES

LEARNING STRATEGIES

➤ Make labels in English for everything in your home. Repeat the new vocabulary every time you look at a label.

➤ With a classmate, describe each room in your home. Then compare your homes.

CITY OR COUNTRY

WARM UP

- Use your picture file or illustrations from newspapers, magazines, real estate ads, or books. Assemble illustrations of different locations (city, coast, small town, farm, country, ranch, mountains, suburbs).
- Ask questions about where people are living in these illustrations. *Is it the city? the country? Do they live on a farm? a ranch? in an apartment?*
- Ask students where they are living now. Do they like it?
- Ask if anyone was born in a rural area. Where? What was it like?
- Ask students to tell you where they enjoy(ed) living most. Why?
- Help with vocabulary. Write new words on the board for students to copy into the **Vocabulary** section of their notebooks.

IN THE TEXT

- Have students look at the illustrations on both pages, or show the transparency with books closed.
- To introduce the vocabulary, see the suggested procedures in **TO THE TEACHER**.
- Discuss each location. Either talk about the places yourself or ask questions for students to answer. For example, talk about the desert. Ask:

  Is it dry or wet in the desert?
  Is it cold or hot in summer in the desert?
  Is it quiet or noisy? Is there a lot of grass?
  Are there cactus plants in the desert?

- Ask students to ask questions about the other illustrations. Have some students ask questions and others answer them.

Partner Interview

- Follow the suggested procedures on page T4.

Group Discussion

OBJECTIVE: To integrate new vocabulary into the context of students' experiences; to listen to other students' experiences and take notes.

- Follow the suggested procedures on page T49, but divide into groups of three rather than five.
- Can any conclusions be drawn? (For example, were more students born in the city than the country? Do a number of students want to live in the same place? etc.)

Speech

OBJECTIVE: To reinforce new vocabulary by using it in a formal presentation to the class; to express preference and use a visual aid.

- For the next class, have students find an illustration or photo of a beautiful place to live.
- *Variation:* Provide the illustrations for the students to choose from.
- Follow the suggested procedures on page T33.
- Have different students tell the class about a place they would like to live. Be sure they show their visual aid with their explanation.

Group Game: *"Gossip!"*

OBJECTIVE: To listen to and repeat a story with details.

- Have students close their books.
- Divide the class into groups of eight.
- Have each group choose a *leader.*
- Have all leaders open their books to **GOSSIP SECRETS** on page 247 in the **student text APPENDIX**, and silently read the appropriate secret several times. Then have the leader close his or her text and whisper the secret to the student sitting next to him or her (Student 1).
- Have Student 1 whisper the secret to the next student (Student 2). Continue until Student 7 hears the secret.
- Have Student 8 in each group write the secret on the board.
- Then read the secret aloud to the whole class:

    I was born and grew up on a farm in the country. It was very peaceful and beautiful. Then I went to the city with my husband. I did not like the city. It was too noisy and crowded. Now my family and I live in a town in the mountains. We are happy there.

- Ask what information was omitted. What was changed? Which group had the best information?

EXPANSION

- Have students role play an interviewer and interviewee about where to live. Assign roles. (For example, the person being interviewed lives in a shack in the desert. The interviewer is a Hollywood talk show host who has flown out to do the interview.) Have students brainstorm questions, which you then write on the board, such as *Where do you live? How long have you been living there? Is it noisy or quiet? Is there pollution?*
- Divide the class into pairs and have them write down the role plays. Give them time to practice, then have several pairs do their role play interviews.
- Ask the class to decide which role play was the funniest, the most creative, used the most new words, etc.

HOMES

WARM UP

- If you can, prepare for this lesson by taking photos of different types of housing around the school neighborhood. If not, use your picture file for different types of homes.
- Distribute the photos or illustrations to different students.
- Give students a few minutes to think about what they want to say. Circulate; help as needed.
- *Variation:* Assemble students into groups of five or six. Have the groups do the activity together and report back to the class.
- Have individual students or a group *reporter* talk for a few minutes about the illustration they have.
- Write new vocabulary on the board for students to copy into the **Vocabulary** section of their notebooks.
- *Variation*: Bring a doll house to class. Either talk about the doll house, using the vocabulary as much as possible, or have students come up and tell you about different things (the **chimney**, **roof**, **porch**, etc.)
- If students can talk about the different rooms, allow them to do so. It would be a good introduction to later lessons in the unit.
- Keep the doll house in class for the duration of the unit. Refer to it as you and the students study the different lessons.

IN THE TEXT

- With the students, look at the illustrations on both pages, or show the transparency with books closed.
- To introduce the vocabulary, see the suggested procedures in **TO THE TEACHER**.
- Ask students to pick a place they *don't* live in. Have them describe what it would be like to live there.
- Write *Where would you like to live?* on the board. With your class, refer to **Polite Expressions** on page 227 of the student text for other examples of *would like*.
- Ask students where they would like to live most; where they would like to live least. Ask *Why?* in both instances.

What's the Story

- Follow the suggested procedures on page T23.

Conversation Squares

OBJECTIVE: To interview classmates about addresses and phone numbers; to make a class directory.

- Practice the interview questions with the students. Be sure they understand the questions and the vocabulary. Supply any additional words needed.
- Divide the class into groups of four.
- Have them write their own names first, and fill in the first blank box about themselves.
- Then have them ask their three partners their names and the questions and fill in the blanks.
- Circulate; help as needed.
- Ask several groups to give their partners' names and addresses and telephone numbers.
- Have all students copy their *own* information on a separate piece of paper and give it to you. Compile an alphabetical list of the class with their names, addresses, and telephone numbers. Distribute the list. Tell the class to use it if they are absent and need to know about the work or if they need any information from a classmate.

EXPANSION

- Get *Change of Address* forms from the post office.
- Distribute them in class.
- Write a new address on the board. Tell the class that everyone is moving to this address and has to inform the post office.
- Have the class fill out the forms with their own names and the new address.
- Circulate; help as needed.

•• Bring in and discuss other forms where addresses are needed.

THE KITCHEN

WARM UP

- Bring in realia in a box with items from the kitchen (for example, a tea kettle, a can opener, a pot, a sugar bowl, a plate, small appliances). Or use items from the kitchen of the doll house.
- Prepare small individual signs: **oven, sink, cabinets, refrigerator, table and chairs, food preparation.**
- Put the realia or models on a table in the front of the classroom.
- Divide the class into six groups; give each group one of the above signs.
- Have each group come up and choose the items that would be classified under that sign. Because there is overlap, limit the number of items they can take.
- Have students arrange the items in their "space."
- When each group finishes their arrangement, have a *reporter* tell the class about their items and what they are used for.
- *Variation*: Give individual students one of the cards and have the student come to the front of the room and choose one item for the category. Give several students a chance to use the same card; then switch.

IN THE TEXT

- With the students, look at the illustrations on both pages of the text or show the transparency with books closed.
- To introduce the vocabulary, see the suggested procedures in **TO THE TEACHER**.

What's the Story?

- Follow the suggested procedures on page T23, but divide into groups of five rather than three.

Partner Game: *"Same or different?"*

OBJECTIVE: To test observation and practice remembering detail.

- Divide the class into pairs.
- Explain that one partner will look at the kitchen on page 66; the other partner will look at the kitchen on page 67.
- Have partners make two lists—one with the heading SAME and one with the heading DIFFERENT—and decide what is the same and what is different in each kitchen.
- When all students have completed their lists, have several pairs report back to the class.
- Who had the longest lists?

EXPANSION

- Bring in less familiar kitchen utensils, such as a radish curler, a garlic press, an apple corer. Ask students what they think the utensils are.
- Have the appropriate food ready to demonstrate how to use the tools.
- Ask students if they have any interesting kitchen tools they can bring in to show.
- Allow students to demonstrate during the next class.

- •• Questions for discussion:

  Do you do the cooking? If not, who does the cooking? How often?
  Do you eat in the kitchen? If not, where do you eat?
  Do you do laundry in the kitchen? If not, where do you do the laundry?
  Do you use canned foods? Which ones? Where do you keep them?
  Do you use frozen foods? Which ones? Where do you keep them?
  Do you make coffee? How do you make coffee?

- ••• Ask students to bring in their coffee makers and prepare coffee for the class, explaining how they do it.

THE DINING ROOM

WARM UP

- Set the table. Bring in: a dinner plate, a salad plate, a dessert plate
  - a soup bowl
  - a cup and saucer
  - a water glass
  - a dinner fork, a dessert fork
  - a soup spoon, a teaspoon
  - a knife
  - a napkin

(You can also extend this list with candlesticks, a tablecloth, a salt and pepper shaker, a serving spoon, a vase and flowers, etc.)

- Either set the table yourself or have all the above waiting to be set.
- Have students tell you what to do, or have a student, in the front of the room, ready to follow instructions to set the table.
- Have several students come up and "sit" at the table and pretend to have dinner. The other students should tell them what to do and say.
- Write key phrases on the board.
- Ask students where they *usually* eat in their homes. Do they put all this on the table? What do they *usually* use? Who do they *usually* eat with? etc.
- Have several students describe how they usually set their tables at home.

IN THE TEXT

- Talk about the illustration on page 68. Ask ***What is happening in the illustration? Who are the people? What are they doing? Is it a weekday or a weekend? What day do you think it is? Why?***
- Point to the individual items in the illustration or on the transparency.
- Have students call out the vocabulary word. Check for pronunciation and understanding.
- Talk about the phrases: ***Pass the butter, please. Set the table. Clear the table. Pour a glass of _____ .***
- This might be an appropriate time to explain ***please*** and ***thank you*** and their appropriate uses in English. When are polite phrases used in students' languages? How are they used?
- As a **Cross-Cultural Exchange**, ask students to teach the class how to say ***please*** and ***thank you*** in their languages.

Partner Interview

- Follow the suggested procedures on page T4.

Group Activity

OBJECTIVE: To compare cultural differences in conversations.

- Divide the class into groups of four or five. Have a cultural mix if possible.
- Have students decide on five things people say at the dinner table in English. Groups should choose a *recorder* to write the list.
- When all students have finished, have each recorder write the list on the board and a member of the same group read the list.
- Compare lists. What was similar? What was different?
- Have students copy the new vocabulary words into the **Vocabulary** section of their notebooks.

Group Role Play

OBJECTIVE: To make group decisions; to write a dialog; to combine verbal and non-verbal simulation.

- Read the instructions with the class and be sure they understand them.
- Have each group decide which scenario to focus on. Have each person in the group pick a role.
- Do some sample dialogs with the class before they attempt to do their own.
- Have the groups write their role plays. Circulate; help as needed.
- Have several groups present their role plays to the class.
- Have students copy new polite phrases into the **Vocabulary** section of their notebooks.
- Discuss any topics that arise during the presentations.

Cross-Cultural Exchange

OBJECTIVE: To discuss traditional customs.

- Use the picture on page 69 as a point of conversation. Ask *Where do you think this meal is taking place? What meal do you think it is? Who are the people? What are they eating and drinking? What do you think they are talking about?* etc.
- Ask about traditional eating customs in the students' countries. It may be appropriate for students from similar backgrounds to form groups and prepare little speeches.
- Draw conclusions. Which countries' customs are similar? Which are different? Why do students think different countries have different customs?

EXPANSION

- Play "True or False." Have students look at the illustration of the dining room for a minute, remembering everything they can. Then have students close their books. Make statements such as *The father is bringing dinner to the table.* Have students call out "true" or "false."
- •• *Variation*: Divide the class into two teams. Give statements and have each team raise their hands when they know if the statement is "true" or "false." If the statement is false, the team has to correct it. If they can't, the other team has the chance to answer.

THE LIVING ROOM

WARM UP

- Use your picture file or bring in magazines with advertisements of furniture.
- Distribute the pictures to the students individually or in groups.
- Tell students they are going to write a description of "their" picture.
- Give them some time to think. Circulate; help as needed.
- Have students write a description of the room, using the vocabulary they know. Allow them to turn to page 70 for vocabulary support.
- Set a time limit (5–10 minutes). When they have finished, have several students show their pictures to the class and describe them.
- Write new vocabulary on the board. Have students copy the vocabulary into the **Vocabulary** section of their notebooks.

IN THE TEXT

- To introduce the vocabulary, see the suggested procedures in **TO THE TEACHER**.
- Talk about the illustration. Ask students what is happening; have each student contribute one line.
- Create a paragraph on the board.
- *Variation:* Divide the class into small groups. Have each group write a paragraph describing the scene. Be sure each student contributes at least one sentence. Have each group read their paragraph, with each student reading the line(s) he or she contributed.

Group Vocabulary Challenge

- Follow the suggested procedures on page T17.

Class Game: *"What do you do in the living room?"*

- Follow the suggested procedures on page T17.

Group Game: *"Gossip!"*

OBJECTIVE: To listen to and repeat a story with details.

- Follow the procedures on page T63.

    I love my living room. I stay in the living room all day. Sometimes I lie on the sofa and watch TV. Sometimes I listen to music and sleep in the armchair. Sometimes I walk on the coffee table and eat the plant there. I like to play with the pillow on the sofa and the lampshade on the lamp. I am a beautiful yellow cat.

- Ask what information was omitted? What was changed? Which group had the best information?

Community Activity

OBJECTIVE: To use outside resources to become familiar with places to buy furniture and with furniture costs.

- Collect circulars and ads that advertise furniture. Bring them to class.
- Distribute the circulars to each student or to groups of students.
- Decide with the class what furniture to put in an empty living room.
- Either draw a floor plan of a living room on the board (windows, doors, etc.) or write the heading LIVING ROOM on the board.
- As students make suggestions, draw the piece of furniture or list it.
- Have students look at their ads and decide where to buy the piece.
- List prices next to the piece of furniture.
- How much will it cost to furnish a living room?
- *Variations*: Have students do this activity in groups, then report back to the class what their decisions are and what the total bill is. Or give the groups or the entire class a budget figure ($2,000) and have them make the decisions based on their budget.

EXPANSION

- Divide the class into groups. Tell them their assignment to research for the next class.
- Have each group visit two furniture stores and price an item. Assign items to the different groups—a sofa, a floor lamp, a table lamp, a coffee table, a rocking chair (new vocabulary), a chair, a cabinet, etc.
- For the next class, have the groups report back. What stores did they visit? What did they find out in their "market research"?

THE BEDROOM

WARM UP

- Bring in realia: an alarm clock, a nightgown (or nightcap!), and a pillow.
- Show the class the realia. Ask what room of the house they think the topic of conversation will be today.
- Ask the students to describe the bedroom of their fantasy. What would it be like if they could design and furnish it? Help with vocabulary and list words as students describe their bedrooms.

IN THE TEXT

- With the students, look at the illustration in the text or have them look at the transparency with the books closed.

- Ask students what they see:

   What is the scene?
   Whose bedroom is it?
   What are the girls doing?
   Who is in the photo on the dresser?
   What music are they listening to?
   Who is talking on the telephone? etc.

- To introduce the vocabulary, see the suggested procedures in **TO THE TEACHER.**

Class Game: *"What do you remember?"*
OBJECTIVE: To test observation and practice remembering detail.

- Have the class look at the illustration on page 72, then close their books.
- Ask students to list everything they can remember about the illustration and to count their items.
- Have students report their lists as you make a list on the board.
- Show the transparency or have students open their texts to page 72.
- Who had the most detailed list?

Partner Interview

- Follow the suggested procedures on page T4.

Draw
OBJECTIVE: To recall a childhood memory; to integrate vocabulary into explaining a drawing.

- Ask students if they remember where they slept as a child. If they had several different homes, have them recall their favorite.
- Have several students tell the class about their childhood bedrooms.
- Write new vocabulary on the board for students to write in the **Vocabulary** section of their notebooks.
- Divide the class into pairs.
- Instruct students to draw a picture of how they recall their childhood bedroom looked. When they are finished, have them tell their partner about the room.
- Have each pair join another pair and share their bedroom pictures and descriptions. Have the group of four decide which *one* bedroom to describe to the entire class. Give each group an opportunity for their *reporter* to tell the class about his or her bedroom.

EXPANSION

- Prepare cards. On one, write a partial definition such as *You hang clothes in it.* On another, write *closet.* Prepare as many cards—and some extras—as there are students in the class (*You sleep in it; bed; It wakes you up in the morning; alarm clock,* etc.).
- Put all the cards in a box. Distribute all cards to the students; then have students ask one another for matching cards.
- Have all students find their partners, sit with them, and then read their card matches to each other. They can also read them to the class.
- •• Have students look at the illustration on page 72 again. Make statements including prepositions of place, such as *It's between the mirror and the comb* (students guess brush); *It's yellow and on the floor* (students guess shirt), etc. Refer to prepositions in **Grammar for Conversation**, page 222 of the **student text**.

THE BATHROOM

WARM UP

- Bring in realia—soap, shampoo, toothbrushes, bath toys, etc. Use your judgment as to whether to bring in items such as toilet paper (remembering that students need this vocabulary too).
- Make a display. Mention the use of the item (*You wash your hair with it*) and have students either call out the item or come up and show it. (At this point, ask what brand the student prefers and why.) Ask questions about cultural differences. *Do children play with bathtub toys in your country? What kind of toys?* etc.

IN THE TEXT

- To introduce the vocabulary, see the suggested procedures in **TO THE TEACHER.**

What's the Story?

- Follow the suggested procedures on page T23.

Cross-Cultural Exchange

OBJECTIVE: To compare bathrooms in different cultures.

- Read the questions or have different students read them.
- Divide the class into groups of four or five.
- If many cultures are represented, one or two students can answer for their group. If all students are from the same country but different cities, they can compare different parts of that country.

EXPANSION

- Discuss more particulars of the bathroom in the illustration. *Where is* the *hot water faucet—on the right or the left? Where is the cold water faucet?*
- Try to elicit more specific vocabulary such as *shower head, spout, toilet tank,* etc.

- •• Ask students which way the water whirls down the sink—clockwise or counterclockwise? Explain the terms *clockwise* and *counterclockwise.* How does it whirl below/above the equator? (Have them check at home or in the rest room and report back!) North of the equator, in the Northern Hemisphere, it whirls clockwise; in the Southern Hemisphere, counterclockwise!

AT HOME

WARM UP

- Bring in pictures showing rooms of the house.
- Talk about each illustration in simple terms: discuss what room it is, what the furniture is, etc.
- *Variation*: Ask students the questions as you point to the items.
- Ask students what rooms are in their homes and what furniture they have in each room. (This is a review of the pages so far.)
- Either list rooms/furniture on the board, or draw a room and its furnishings as a student describes his/her home.
- Ask students what their favorite room is in their home and why.

IN THE TEXT

- Look at the illustration with the students or show the transparency.
- To introduce the vocabulary, see the suggested procedures in **TO THE TEACHER**.

Class Vocabulary Challenge

OBJECTIVE: To review the vocabulary with the class.

- Leave the transparency up. Have students use a page in the **Vocabulary** section of their notebooks and write down all the vocabulary they can remember, using the illustration as a prompt, or from memory. Tell the class to number the words they remember.
- Give a five-minute time frame. Then have individual students tell the class how many words they remembered.
- Have several students read their lists to the class.
- Instruct students to add new vocabulary to their lists.

Group Survey

- Follow the suggested procedures on page T19.

EXPANSION

- Ask students about homes in their countries or cities. Similarities? Differences?

NEIGHBORS

WARM UP

- If you can locate a video of a TV show such as *The Honeymooners*, *All in the Family*, or any short clip showing episodes with neighbors, show the video or clip and talk about the American concept of neighbors.
- Have students talk about what a good neighbor is. What do they think a bad neighbor is?
- Who has good neighbors? Who has bad neighbors? Have students compare their experiences and even give each other advice.

IN THE TEXT

- With the students, look at the illustrations on both pages of the text or show the transparencies with books closed.
- Tell one story about one illustration. Then have students tell other stories about the other illustrations.
- List new vocabulary on the board as the stories are being told. Most of the vocabulary in the text should be generated as well as the extra words.
- Suggest to students that they write the new words in their texts.
- To introduce the vocabulary, see the suggested procedures in **TO THE TEACHER.**

Partner Interview

- Follow the suggested procedures on page T4.

Group Role Play

OBJECTIVE: To make group decisions and write a group dialog about neighbors; to combine verbal and nonverbal simulation.

- Divide the class into groups of four or five.
- Have each group select a scene on pages 76 and 77. Try to ensure that each scene is represented.
- Have each group write a script for a conversation. Be sure roles are included for everyone.
- Circulate; help as needed.
- Have all the groups take turns presenting their conversations to the class.

EXPANSION

- Ask about the students' concept of neighbors. What is different where they live now from where they grew up? What do they like/dislike about each experience?

PROBLEMS AT HOME

WARM UP

- Bring in what you can for realia: insect/ant spray, a mouse trap, spackle and a scraper, a pail, a plunger, gloves and a hat. Also bring in a telephone to make a phone call.
- Tell students that the class is going to play a pantomime game. Either in groups or as individuals, have students pick a prop and pantomime the problem.
- Have the class guess what the problem is. The one who guesses uses the telephone to call the exterminator, repairman, plumber, etc.
- Discuss solutions to the problems as students guess the correct answers.

IN THE TEXT

- Instead of going over the vocabulary first, have students start by doing the **Group Problem Posing/Problem Solving** activity. (They should have had practice from the **WARM UP**.)
- Review the vocabulary next, following the procedures in **TO THE TEACHER**.

Group Problem Posing/Problem Solving

OBJECTIVE: To come to group consensus about stating a problem; to arrive at a group solution for the stated problem.

- Divide the class into groups of five. Have each group pick a *reporter*.
- Instruct the groups to decide what the problem is in each of the scenes on page 78.
- Have the groups make one statement of advice, and suggest a solution for each problem.
- Have each reporter state the problem and the solution to the class.
- Compare solutions. Have the class decide which solution was best for each problem.

Group Role Play

OBJECTIVE: To make group decisions and write a group dialog about problems in the home; to combine verbal and non-verbal communication practice.

- Divide the class into groups of five.
- Have each group select one scene on page 78. Have students narrate the scenes. Try to ensure that each scene is represented.
- Follow the suggested procedures on page T69.

Strip Stories

OBJECTIVE: To state problems; to find solutions.

- Look at each strip story separately. Use the open texts or the transparency.
- Ask what is happening. Have students state the problem first and then tell you the mistakes that are being made.
- Decide with the class what to write under each illustration. Write on the transparency or on the board. Supply vocabulary as needed. Have the students copy the captions into their texts or into the **Activities** section of their notebooks.
- *Variation*: Have students do the activity in small groups.

Group Activity

OBJECTIVE: To find solutions to problems at home.

- Have students remain in their same groups.
- Have the students choose a *recorder* and a *reporter*.
- Ask them to brainstorm all the problems they have at home and have the recorder make a group list.
- When all the groups have finished the task, have each reporter read the group's list to the class. As the reporters are reading, write the lists on the board. Keep track of the repeated problems.
- Decide together which problem is the biggest one and what to do about all of them.
- Have students copy new words in the **Vocabulary** section of their notebooks.

EXPANSION

- Bring in classified advertisements for plumbers, electricians, exterminators, etc. Ask the class when they would call these people.
- Role play the telephone conversations.

REVIEW

IN THE TEXT

Partner Interview
- Follow the suggested procedures on page T4.

Write
OBJECTIVE: To transfer oral information to written form.
- Have students do their individual journal writing.

Tell the Class
- Follow the suggested procedures on page T7.

EXPANSION
- In the **Journal** section of their notebooks, have students write about another aspect of the **HOMES** unit—a favorite room, a favorite activity, problems they have with a neighbor, etc.
- Instruct them to use page 80 as a model to set up their free-writing journal.
- Have several students read their journal entries.

- •• Review all illustrations or show the transparencies from **Unit 5** again.
- Have students make up questions about the illustrations. Write their questions on the board.
- Have individual students choose a question and ask either a specific student or anyone in the class.
- When that student answers, he/she asks the next question

UNIT TEST
- A **conversation test** and a **vocabulary test** for this unit are located in the back of this Teacher's Guide, plus suggestions for administration. Feel free to make as many copies as you need.

UNIT 6

SHOPPING

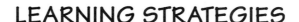

LEARNING STRATEGIES

➤ Write all your shopping lists in English. Go shopping with a friend from class. Shop in English.

➤ Show your purchases to classmates. Describe your purchases in English. Ask questions about what your classmates bought.

GOING SHOPPING

WARM UP

- Collect ads and circulars from as many stores in your community as possible (newspaper inserts are a good source). You will need them for this entire unit, in one form or another.
- Show some of the ads (without the names of the stores) to the students; ask if they know which stores the ads are from. What is sold in each store? Don't show them the names of the stores yet.
- Bring in items from home that you could buy in different stores. Ask the class *What's this?* (sandals, aspirin, nails, etc.) and *Where do you buy* (sandals, aspirin, nails, etc.)*?*
- Point to items students are wearing (or have with them), and ask *What's this?* and *Where did you buy it?*
- Point to objects around the classroom and ask *What's this?* and *Where can you buy it?*

IN THE TEXT

- With the students, look at the illustrations on pages 82 and 83 of the text or have them look at the transparency with books closed.
- To introduce the vocabulary, follow the procedures in **TO THE TEACHER**.
- Point to each store and ask *What kind of store is this?* (Point out that *shop* is another word for *store*.)
- Ask if the students go to a *mall* or a *shopping center*. Write the names of the malls or shopping centers on the board. Ask *Is it a good mall/shopping center? Do you like it? Why?/Why not?* Allow students to discuss their favorites. If there are no malls or shopping centers in your community, ask students if they have ever seen a mall or shopping center, and where they have seen one (in a movie? in another country?).
- Ask how this mall/shopping center is different from the ones they know (indoor/outdoor, one-story/two-story, bigger/smaller, more crowded, etc.).
- Write the differences on the board.

Class Activity

OBJECTIVE: To reinforce vocabulary, introduce names of local stores, and integrate the vocabulary with students' experiences at local stores.

- Read the instructions aloud. Then ask *Is there a coffee shop in your neighborhood? What's the name of the coffee shop?*
- Write the name of a coffee shop in the space provided on page 83. Continue with each of the other stores. If there is no local example, write the generic name of the store on the store sign.
- Whenever the students mention more than one of a kind of store, write all the store names on the board and ask *How many of you shop at this pharmacy? How many shop at this one? Why?* Have each student write the name of the one he or she prefers in the space provided in his or her text.
- Ask *What do you buy at the pharmacy?* Have individual students give responses and write them on the board.
- Ask questions about the neighborhood stores:

  Do people speak English in the store?
  Do they speak your native language?
  Do they speak another language?
  Did you ever have a communication problem in a store?
  What happened?
  How did you solve it?

Group Discussion

OBJECTIVE: To talk about shopping in your community; to ask questions, answer, and listen to answers.

- Follow the suggested procedures on page T49.
- When the groups finish the answers to questions 1–3, they must decide on whole-group answers to questions 4 and 5.
- When all groups are finished, have them report their group's answers to questions 4 and 5 to the class.

EXPANSION

- Use the circulars. Give each group a circular and have them make up a wish list of things they would like to buy. They must answer these questions: *What is the item? How much does it cost? Who is it for?*

- •• Ask students about stores in their native countries or cities: *Are they like stores in the United States/Canada? How are they the same/different? Are prices higher/lower? What can you buy in stores in your native country that you can't buy here?*

SPORTING GOODS STORE

WARM UP

- Bring in as much sports realia as you can: running shoes, golf clubs, tennis racquets, basketball, fishing flies, etc.
- Arrange the equipment on a desk or table before class.
- When students arrive, ask each one (or a group, depending on the size of the class) to choose one item. Each student should get a turn to say something about the item he or she chose, even if just to name the item or say what color it is. Students who can say more may do so.
- Ask students if they play any of the sports. Which ones? In what seasons do they play? Who do they play with? Do they play on teams? What equipment do they use? Where do they get their equipment? Do they buy any of it themselves? Where?
- Elicit as much vocabulary as you can before you open books or show the transparencies. Write the new words on the board for students to copy into the **Vocabulary** section of their notebooks.

IN THE TEXT

- To introduce the vocabulary, follow the procedures in **TO THE TEACHER**.
- Point to each piece of athletic equipment and ask *What kind of equipment is this?* Point to each of the items again and ask students *What do you do with this?* Elicit action vocabulary. You may need to model an answer for the students *What do you do with a baseball? You throw it.* Write the action vocabulary on the board; have students copy the vocabulary in the lines provided in the text or into the **Vocabulary** section of their notebooks.

Class Discussion

OBJECTIVE: To talk about buying athletic equipment; to answer questions, to listen to answers, and draw conclusions.

- Follow the suggested procedures on page T29.
- You might want to write these headings on the board: FAVORITE SPORT, STORE, ITEM, COST, and ATHLETIC CLOTHING. Have a student volunteer to write on the board. Ask the class each of the five discussion questions, and have the student at the board list each item that is mentioned.
- Draw conclusions at the end of the discussion from the information listed.
- *Variation:* Ask students to draw conclusions.

Group Decision

OBJECTIVE: To explain a choice, agree, and disagree in English.

- Divide the class into groups of four and have each group choose one of the three situations. Tell them to discuss possible items to buy and decide on one as a group.
- Write on the board **ITEM:** *What will you buy?* **COST**: *What will it cost? STORE: Where will you buy it?* **REASON**: *Why did you choose this item?*
- Tell the groups they will have to report answers to these four questions to the class.
- When the group discussions are finished, have the *reporter* from each group give the group's answers.

Group Vocabulary Challenge

- Follow the suggested procedures on page T17.
- When the pairs have finished, have students read the matching pairs for the class.

Find Someone Who

- Follow the suggested procedures on page T12.

EXPANSION

- Ask what sports girls/women play in the students' cultures. Is this changing? How?

•• Play a pantomime game. Start by pantomiming a sport. Whoever guesses the sport takes the next turn.

••• Role play a scene in a sporting goods store with a sales clerk and a customer who wants to buy an item from the **Group Decision** activity. Two students from each of the original groups can volunteer (or be chosen) to play the roles. Or students can write their names on slips of paper, which they fold and give to you. Mix up the pile of papers, then have a student pick two slips to determine who will play roles.

TOY STORE

WARM UP

- Bring in as many toys as you can. Pass them out at random and tell students to examine them and pass them around.
- Write these headings on the board: TOY, COST, and AGE. Ask the student holding each toy at that moment to tell what the toy is, how much it might cost, and what age child would like it. Have other students help with the answers as needed. Write the information under the appropriate heading on the board.
- Have the students holding the toys pass the toys to other students.
- Ask a new group of students to bring the toys to the front of the room. One by one, have them demonstrate to the class how to play with the toy. (The demonstration may be pantomimed with an accompanying explanation.)
- If a student has trouble with the demonstration, have another student come up to help.

IN THE TEXT

- To introduce the vocabulary, follow the procedures in **TO THE TEACHER**.
- Point out that some pictured toys do not have corresponding words because the words have already been introduced on an earlier page. Ask the students if they can remember which words they have already studied and what page they were on. If students remember *baseball, football,* and *bathtub toys,* but not the pages they were on, have them look up the words in the **student text Alphabetical Word List to Picture Dictionary**, page 250, which lists the picture dictionary page for each word.
- Ask *How many students had a (teddy bear, toy truck, paint set,* etc.), and have students raise their hands. Have students count the numbers in English, but don't write them on the board. At the end of the vocabulary practice, ask which toy was the most popular in the class. See if students can remember the numbers.
- Ask students what age child would be interested in each toy.
- Ask what you can do with each toy in the illustration.

Partner Interview

- Follow the suggested procedures for **Partner Interview** on page T4.

Group Decision

OBJECTIVE: To include everyone in the decision-making process, and to use new vocabulary in the context of a discussion.

- Have the students make a list of appropriate toys for each of the five children.
- Divide the class into groups of four. Tell students that everyone in the group must share their list and suggest a toy for each of the five children. Then the group must decide together which toys to buy.
- When groups have all decided, list the five different ages on the board, and ask groups what they decided.
- Have a student list the decisions on the board.
- What was the most popular toy?

Group Survey

- Follow the suggested procedures on page T19.
- Review the past tense question form with *did*.

EXPANSION

- Ask students what toys children play with in their native countries.
- •• Have students describe their favorite childhood toy to the class.

SHOE STORE

WARM UP

- Take a quick look at students' shoes and your own. Ask students with different kinds of shoes to come to the front of the room and show their shoes. (Don't embarrass students with worn-out shoes!)
- As different shoes are demonstrated, write the kind of shoes on the board. For example, students may have *loafers, flats, boots,* etc. You may want to review shoes found on other pages of the text, such as pages 9 and 84.
- Talk about the shoes: *What color are they? Describe them.* Write relevant vocabulary on the board and have students copy the vocabulary on the lines provided in the text or into the **Vocabulary** section of their notebooks.

IN THE TEXT

- To introduce the vocabulary, follow the procedures in **TO THE TEACHER**.
- You may want to discuss shoe sizes in the United States. Also, use students' shoes as examples of different types of materials used.

Group Role Play

OBJECTIVE: To create a conversation for a shoe-shopping situation, and to combine verbal and nonverbal communication.

- You may need to demonstrate this role play with students before they attempt it. If you do, play one role (a sales person) and have two students play the other roles (a customer and a friend).
- Divide the class into groups of five. You may want to help students choose roles (two salesmen, the male customer, the female customer, and her friend).
- Have students write a conversation.
- When students have completed their role plays and practiced them, have each group demonstrate their role play for another group.
- Then have two or three groups present their role plays for the whole class.

Find Someone Who

OBJECTIVE: To review classmates' names and share personal information; to ask conversation questions about shoes.

- Follow the suggested procedures on page T12.
- When everyone (or almost everyone) is done, ask the class *who* questions: *Who has more than ten pairs of shoes? Who wants cowboy boots?* etc. (Put these five *who* questions on the board while the students are talking; fill in names from the students' answers.)

Group Discussion

OBJECTIVE: To integrate new vocabulary into the context of students' experiences; to listen to other students' experiences and take notes.

- Follow the suggested procedures on page T49.
- Because of the number of questions, you might want to have individual students in each group be responsible for one or two questions.
- After groups have completed their discussion, go over the questions.
- If time is short, you may ask each group one or two questions.
- Pay particular attention to 8: students may be confused by U.S. sizing, since it may be different in their countries.

Cross-Cultural Exchange

OBJECTIVE: To compare sizes and kinds of shoes in different countries.

- Follow the suggested procedures on page 74.

EXPANSION

- Discuss with students *What shoes are appropriate to wear to work? to school? dancing? at home? in cold weather? in warm weather?*

MEN'S CLOTHING STORE

WARM UP

- Use the ads and circulars collected for **GOING SHOPPING**. Pass them out as students come into the classroom, and have students find men's clothing ads and list the different kinds of clothing for sale. As other students arrive, have them join the informal groups. When class starts, have the groups read their lists to the class and write the vocabulary on the board.
- Have the men in the class come to the front of the room, and ask the class *What are they wearing?*
- Check off every item on the board that is actually being worn by a student in the class. (If there are no men in class, have students describe clothing worn by relatives or use the pictures in the text.)

IN THE TEXT

- To introduce the vocabulary, follow the procedures in **TO THE TEACHER**.

Partner Interview

- Follow the suggested procedures on page T4.

Group Decision

OBJECTIVE: To discuss and decide as a group what the men will want to wear.

- Divide the class into groups of five or six; try to include both men and women in each group. If possible, have each group also use a circular with men's clothing for suggestions.
- Have each group select a *reporter*.
- Tell the groups you want them to decide what the men in the picture will want to buy and wear for each activity. Tell the men to think about themselves, and the women to think about the men in their family.
- When the discussions are finished, have the reporter report the discussion results to the class.

EXPANSION

- Have the same groups look at the circulars to decide if they advertise any good buys in men's clothing, and report the sales to the class. Decide which are the best buys.

- • Have each of the men in the class make a speech about his favorite piece of clothing. The speech should include when and where he got the clothing, whether he bought it himself or someone gave it to him, and why he likes it so much. If possible, students should wear the clothing during their speeches.

WOMEN'S CLOTHING STORE

WARM UP

- Ask students to bring circulars to class, other ads for women's clothing, or a mail order catalog. Bring as many as possible yourself.
- Write these questions on the board: *Do men or women spend more money on clothing? Who likes to shop for clothing more, men or women?*
- Poll the students for their opinions. Is there a class consensus? Ask the students *Why?* Elicit as many reasons in support of their opinions as possible.

IN THE TEXT

- Everyone will notice immediately that most of the items in the illustration are not in the vocabulary box on this page. Explain that much of the vocabulary here is a review, and that they will be practicing it in a partner activity.
- If appropriate, use the **student text Alphabetical Word List to Picture Dictionary**, page 250, to review the vocabulary.
- To introduce the vocabulary, follow the procedures in **TO THE TEACHER**.

Partner Vocabulary Challenge

OBJECTIVE: To review vocabulary for women's clothing.

- Divide the class into pairs; if possible, pair a man and a woman for this activity.
- Instruct students to make one list per pair of words for the Women's Clothing Store picture.

Group Decision

OBJECTIVE: To compare ideas about appropriate clothing for honeymoons, and review women's clothing and costs.

- Read the instructions with the class and make sure they understand what they have to decide on.
- Divide the class into groups. Have each group select a *reporter*. Have each group plan a honeymoon wardrobe for one of the women in the picture.
- When the groups are finished, have reporters tell their group's decisions to the class.

Community Activity

OBJECTIVE: To check women's clothing costs in local stores.

- Depending on how many circulars and ads you have, work individually, in pairs, or in groups, choosing and pricing an item to buy. Have two students help list items and prices on the board. Draw conclusions.
- Have students copy any important information into the **Community** section of their notebooks.

EXPANSION

- Ask how many students in the class like to dress up. What occasions do they dress up for? What do they wear?
- •• Go back to the Group Decision in **MEN'S CLOTHING**. Ask the women in the class what they would buy to wear for each activity.

DEPARTMENT STORE

WARM UP

- Have students look around the classroom and list on the board all the things they see—on the walls, on the floor, on the ceiling, on their desks, on themselves.
- Go down the list with the students, asking *Can you buy this in a department store?* Check all "yes items."
- Look at the checked items again and ask *What department can you buy this in?* When students know, write the name of the department next to the item.
- Ask *How many students shop in a department store?* Make a list on the board of advantages and disadvantages of department store shopping where you live.
- Have students copy any important information into the **Community** section of their notebooks.

IN THE TEXT

- A lot of vocabulary accompanies this illustration. Depending upon the level of your class, you may choose to use all the vocabulary or pick the more common words.
- Look at the illustrations on both pages of the text or show the transparency with students' books closed. Point to each department and ask *Which department is this?*
- To introduce the vocabulary, follow the suggested procedures in **TO THE TEACHER**.
- Ask what you can buy in each department. Write new words on the transparency or the board.
- Discuss *store directory, escalator, elevator,* and *customer service counter.*

Class Discussion

OBJECTIVE: To relate department store vocabulary to students' personal experience.

- Follow the suggested procedures on page T29.
- Ask the questions with the whole class. Be sure to give accurate information about the department stores that are accessible to students.
- If students shop at more than one department store, have them compare stores: prices, quality of merchandise, service, convenience.
- Have different students describe department stores in their native countries.

Partner Game: *"What do you remember?"*

OBJECTIVE: To test observation and practice remembering detail.

- Follow the suggested procedures on page T35.

Partner Role Play

OBJECTIVE: To ask for and give directions in a department store.

- Divide the class into pairs, preferably with new partners.
- Read the instructions aloud and check for comprehension.
- Create a sample conversation with the class, write it on the board, and have students copy it before creating their own.

    Customer: *Excuse me, where's the gift wrap counter?*
    Sales person: *It's right behind you, by the exit.*

- *Review prepositions of place for this role play.*
- Depending on the level of your class, you may assign from one to five of the situations to each pair.
- Give students time to write their role-play conversation and practice it.
- Circulate; help as needed.
- When all the pairs have created at least one conversation, have them join another pair and present their conversations for each other.
- Select several pairs to role play one of the situations in front of the whole class.
- Write new vocabulary on the board. Have students copy the new vocabulary into the **Vocabulary** section of their notebooks.

EXPANSION

- Bring in circulars from area department stores and discuss which ones have good buys. Compare prices of items at department stores and other stores selling similar things.

- ● Take a class field trip to a department store. Have students make a list of all the departments in the store and copy it into the **Community** section of their notebooks. Have each student ask directions to a department. After the trip, compare department lists and experiences asking directions.

- ● ● Ask if anyone in the class has a department store credit card. Bring in credit card applications from department stores. Read the applications together and discuss the rules governing the use of the cards and the advantages and disadvantages of having a department store credit card. Include credit rating, finance charges, interest rate, minimum payment, date due, bad credit, etc.

FLOWER SHOP

WARM UP

- Bring in any real (or artificial) flowers and plants. (Or use pictures of flowers and plants; a seed catalog is a good resource.)
- Ask students if they know the names of the flowers and plants. Ask what the words for the vocabulary are in the students' native languages.
- Ask students what their favorite flower is. Why do they like it? Can they describe it—color, size, scent, leaves, etc.?

IN THE TEXT

- To introduce the vocabulary, follow the procedures in **TO THE TEACHER**.
- Tell stories about the people at the flower shop.
- Explain the custom of giving/sending flowers for different occasions. Point out the ribbons with the sentiments on them: *Happy Birthday, Sympathy* (always difficult for students to understand), *Best Wishes, Get Well, Congratulations*.
- Talk about the new custom of giving and sending balloons.
- Ask students about customs they are familiar with.

What's the Story?

OBJECTIVE: To create a group story using flower-buying situations and vocabulary.

- Divide the class into groups of three or four.
- Read the instructions with the class. Make sure the students understand that each group will create a different story using flower-buying situations, and that they must include all five people in the illustration on page 94 (the customers and the employees) in their story.
- Follow the suggested procedures on page T23.

Partner Role Play

OBJECTIVE: To write and perform a role play in which to review new vocabulary and structures in a given context.

- Follow the suggested procedures on page T55.

Class Discussion

OBJECTIVE: To integrate new vocabulary into the context of students' experiences; to listen to other students' experiences and take notes.

- Follow the suggested procedures on page T29.
- Take notes on this class discussion, and suggest that the students take notes, too.
- Write five headings on the board: FAVORITE FLOWERS, OCCASIONS, FLORISTS, SEND FLOWERS, NATIVE COUNTRY OCCASIONS. As you ask questions and the students answer, put their answers in columns under each heading. Encourage the students to do likewise.
- When the discussion is finished, orally recap the notes on the board, and ask students to summarize the discussion.

EXPANSION

- Some flower names are also used as women's names in English. Make a list on the board of all such names the students can think of: *Daisy, Rose, Lily, Dahlia,* etc. Ask if any of those flower names are also women's names in students' native languages. Write women's "flower names" from all the students' languages on the board and practice pronouncing them. Do any of the students in the class have "flower names"?

- •• Bring in a telephone directory, or make copies of florist pages from a phone directory. Which Yellow Pages ads have FTD logos? What do the logos mean? Has anyone in the class ever wired flowers? How? For what occasion? Where did they have the flowers sent? How did they choose the flowers? Have students copy the information into the **Community** section of their notebooks.

PHARMACY

WARM UP

- Bring in realia: band aids, toothbrushes, baby lotions, cough syrup, etc.
- Set up a "drugstore" before students get to class.
- Ask volunteers to come up and "shop" for things they need.
- Play the role of "interviewer"—ask the shopper what he or she is buying, what brand it is, what it costs. Ask why the student is buying the items.
- Repeat to the class what you have been told. Show the items to the class as though you were doing a spoof on a commercial.

IN THE TEXT

- If students can't handle all the vocabulary on this page; emphasize only the most common words.
- Look at the illustration in the text or show the transparency with students' books closed. Talk about the illustration, pointing out the most common words first. Then go back and talk about the more specific words (*lipstick, nail polish*, etc.). Point out that *drugstore* is another word for *pharmacy*.
- Talk about what the pharmacist is doing (she is filling a prescription for a customer).
- Discuss the role of the pharmacist in other countries. How do pharmacists' roles differ in your students' countries? Can pharmacists dispense medicine without prescriptions? What medicines? Do they give injections?
- Ask what the different customers are doing in the pharmacy in the illustration.

Group Vocabulary Challenge

- Follow the suggested procedures on page T17.
- At the end of this activity, do not erase the list from the board.

Class Survey

OBJECTIVE: To relate vocabulary to students' personal experiences.

- For this activity, use the list already on the board from the **Group Vocabulary Challenge**.
- Ask how many students buy each item listed on the board.
- As students raise their hands, write the number of students next to each item.
- What do most students buy? Have students draw conclusions from the numbers on the list.
- Ask students where they shop for drugstore needs. What is the best drugstore in the community? Are there other places to buy certain items for less money (discount stores)? Where do students prefer to shop? Why?
- Do students have problems with language at the drugstore? What do they do? Have students tell the class their stories.

Conversation Squares

OBJECTIVE: To interview classmates about favorite brands of drugstore items.

- Follow the suggested procedures on page T33.
- Have groups report their brands to the class. Discuss generic brands, store brands, and national brands.

Community Activity

OBJECTIVE: To compare prices in the community.

- Before students "go out" to do this activity, be sure they understand the chart. Explain it with some examples.
- Assign groups of students to do this "market research" between class sessions. Have students go to two different stores to compare prices.
- Students should use the chart in the text to record their findings.
- For the next class, have students report back with the results of their research.
- What conclusions do students draw? Which store has the best prices? Which has the best selection?
- Have students copy any important information into the **Community** section of their notebooks.

EXPANSION

- Have students bring in a sample of their favorite brand of some drugstore item: tissues, hair spray, toothpaste, etc. Have them demonstrate how they use the item and have them tell the class why they prefer this brand.

- • Have groups of students prepare a commercial for a particular brand of a drugstore item and present it to the class as a role play. Encourage them to sing a song in their commercial.

JEWELRY STORE

WARM UP

- Admire a student's piece of jewelry and say *(Lin) has a beautiful ring. It is gold and it has a pearl.* Write the vocabulary on the board. Repeat this activity with other students in the class.
- Talk about your own jewelry. Describe it, tell who gave it to you, and tell what it means to you.

IN THE TEXT

- To introduce the vocabulary, see the suggested procedures in **TO THE TEACHER**.
- Ask about engagement ring and wedding ring customs in students' countries. *Who wears an engagement ring? What finger are engagement and/or wedding rings worn on? Are other engagement jewelry presents traditional?*
- Ask about the illustration again *How do the people feel? Why?*

Group Role Play

OBJECTIVE: To create a story and role play it with a group.

- Divide the class into groups of five or six students. All students will need to play a role.
- Each group makes up a story about one "set" of people; then they write a conversation. Each group selects a *narrator* to tell the audience what is happening. Have students write an ending to their group story. What happens after the people leave the jewelry store?
- When all groups have finished, have them present their role plays for the class.

Partner Interview

- Follow the suggested procedures on page T4.

EXPANSION

- Have students tell the class about a piece of jewelry that has special meaning for them.

HARDWARE STORE

WARM UP

- Bring in as much realia as you can, plus flyers from hardware stores.
- Display the items.
- Ask a volunteer to choose a tool and demonstrate its use. Ask the class what the volunteer is holding and doing.

IN THE TEXT

- To introduce the vocabulary, see the suggested procedures in **TO THE TEACHER**.
- There is a lot of vocabulary in this illustration. Ask students which words they think are the most important to remember, and why.

Class Discussion

OBJECTIVE: To listen to other students' experiences and take notes.

- Ask the questions in the text, and list on the board the names of different hardware stores and items students buy there.
- If a few students know more than the others, have those students be a resource of information for the class.

Partner Activity

OBJECTIVE: To make up a story with a partner, using new vocabulary.

- Read aloud the instructions and questions to the class and check for comprehension.
- Divide the class into pairs. Have the pairs answer each question and write their answers.
- When all the pairs are finished, have them report their answers to the class. If there is not enough time for all answers, ask each pair to answer one question for the class.

Class Game: *"Mime"*

OBJECTIVE: To review new vocabulary with gestures.

- First pantomime the use of a tool yourself. Ask the students what tool you are using.
- When a student guesses, have the student come to the front of the class and pantomime using another tool.
- Depending on how familiar your students are with this vocabulary, you may ask them to close their texts for this activity or use their texts for help.

EXPANSION

- Pass out the hardware store flyers to groups of students. Have the students find "good buys" in the flyers and tell the class about them.
- Write the stores, the items, and their prices on the board. Decide together which stores have the best buys.

OFFICE SUPPLY STORE

WARM UP

- Bring office supplies to class in a bag. Ask students *What do you need in an office?* As students give ideas, write them on the board and have students see if they are in the bag.
- Talk about where to keep supplies: inside a desk drawer? on top of the desk? Where do students keep their office supplies at home? Do they have an office or study corner?

IN THE TEXT

- To introduce the vocabulary, see the suggested procedures in **TO THE TEACHER**.
- Ask if students ever shop in an office supply store. If not, where do they buy pens, cards, etc.? What cards do they buy?

Class Discussion

OBJECTIVE: To describe the function of office supplies.

- Ask students what they do with each item (*staple papers with a stapler,* etc.).
- *Variation:* Do this activity in groups, and have groups report their lists to the class.
- List uses on the board, and have students copy the words and their uses into the **Vocabulary** section of their notebooks.

Find Someone Who

- Follow the suggested procedures on page T12.

Group Activity

OBJECTIVE: To review vocabulary with students' own supplies.

- Divide the class into groups of four or five.
- Have students in each group put all the office supplies they have with them on a desk, list the supplies, and read the list to the class. Compare lists.

EXPANSION

- Assign students to visit two local stores that sell office supplies. Have the students compare the price of notebooks, pens, pencils, paper clips, scotch tape, etc. Ask students to report back in the next class. (They can copy a chart similar to the one on page 97 into the **Community** section of their notebooks.)
- •• Play "20 Questions" with office supplies in the classroom.

ELECTRONICS STORE

WARM UP

- If you have this realia, bring in (or ask students to bring) a CD, an LP record, a cassette tape, a VCR tape, a floppy disk. Bring ads for electronics equipment.
- Play some music. Ask whether students prefer CDs or cassettes. Why?
- Pass out the ads. Ask if students see any good buys.

IN THE TEXT

- To introduce the vocabulary, see the suggested procedures in **TO THE TEACHER**.
- Ask students if they have ever had any problems with any of this electronic equipment. Have them tell stories to the class.

Group Decision

OBJECTIVE: To determine good local prices for equipment.

- Divide the class into groups of five or six. Make flyers and ads available to the groups as resources.
- Depending on time constraint and student interest, limit the activity to certain items, rather than pricing all items in the picture.
- When the groups are finished, have them report, item by item, and compare prices.

Class Discussion

OBJECTIVE: To integrate new vocabulary into the context of students' experiences; to listen to other students' experiences and take notes.

- Write headings on the board: HAVE, WANT, LIKE TO USE, USE AT WORK.
- Ask students the first three questions and list on the board all the kinds of electronic equipment that anyone has, wants, likes to use, or uses at work. Have students draw conclusions about their class and electronic equipment.
- Ask the fourth question. If there are students from many countries in your class, have one or two students tell about popular kinds of electronic equipment in their countries, and kinds of equipment that many people have in their homes, schools, offices, and stores. Compare use in different countries.

EXPANSION

- Have pairs of students role play shopping scenes between a salesclerk and an unhappy customer in an electronics store. The customer is complaining about a piece of electronic equipment purchased in the store that isn't working correctly.

SALES AND ADVERTISEMENTS

WARM UP

- Have students bring in flyers and ads for sales, and use the ones from earlier classes in this unit. Make sure every student or group of students has a flyer.
- Ask students what kinds of sales are advertised in their flyers. Students may answer simply with the names of items for sale. If there are different kinds of sales (white sales, seasonal sales, etc.), write the vocabulary on the board and explain it.

IN THE TEXT

- Look at the illustrations on both pages of the text, or show the transparency with student books closed.
- The vocabulary and concepts in this illustration are complex and will probably need explanation and discussion as you introduce them. (For example: Ask when seasonal sales take place. What is on sale? You may want to list them on the board.) Instead of pointing to the picture and asking for the word, point to the word and ask students to point out an example in the illustrations.
- Ask students to describe what is happening in each illustration. If they use any additional vocabulary, write the words on the board and have students copy the vocabulary in the lines provided in the text or in the **Vocabulary** section of their notebook.
- Ask students if they have ever been to a yard sale. What did they buy? Have they ever had a yard sale (or a church rummage sale and other similar sales)?
- Ask students if they have ever bought anything on layaway, on credit, or with a rain check. What did they buy? Have them describe the process to the class. List the steps of each process on the board.

Strip Stories

OBJECTIVE: To describe strip stories using new vocabulary; to relate vocabulary to students' experiences.

- Have students look at the strip stories with the student sitting next to them, and together decide on possible captions for the stories.
- Ask the class what is happening in each illustration. On the board write different ways of describing the illustrations and captioning them.
- Ask if anyone ever had a bad experience at a clearance sale or when buying a used car. If so, have them tell their stories to the class. Encourage other students to ask questions.

Group Discussion

OBJECTIVE: To integrate vocabulary into students' experiences.

- Follow the suggested procedures on page T49.
- Write these headings on the board: LIKE TO SHOP, BOUGHT ON SALE, GOOD SALES, and BE CAREFUL. Ask how many students like to shop at sales, put the numbers under LIKE TO SHOP, and have students add the total.
- Ask each of the other questions and fill in columns under each heading.
- Have students draw conclusions.

Community Activity

OBJECTIVE: To review sale vocabulary and relate to current sales and student preferences.

- Take out the flyers from the **WARM UP** again. Ask students to look over their flyers and find a sale they are interested in. Ask several students what sale they chose and why they chose it.
- Ask the rest of the class if those sales sound good. Organize this activity in groups: read flyers, select sale items, and report as a group.
- Poll the class. Ask the students *If you see something you really need at a good sale price, will you buy it on credit? Why or why not?* Discuss and list on the board the advantages and disadvantages of credit buying in this or any situation.

EXPANSION

- From the board list of credit advantages and disadvantages, have groups of students choose one. Have the groups create a role play illustrating the advantage or disadvantage, and have each group present their role play for the class.

- • Have students bring something to class that they don't want anymore. Have a class rummage sale: sell to each other or to other classes in the building. Use your class profits to pay for a special class activity (a party, a field trip, etc.).

- • • As an alternative to a rummage sale, put on a class auction. Have everyone in the class take turns being the auctioneer.

REVIEW

IN THE TEXT

Group Decision

OBJECTIVE: To work as a group to decide how to spend $1,000.

- Divide the class into groups of five. Read the instructions aloud, and make sure everyone understands. You may need to give several examples of ways to spend the $1,000. Have students make suggestions.
- Give the groups a time limit: 10 or 15 minutes. Circulate; help as needed.
- When the groups are finished, have each group report their decisions.

Partner Activity

OBJECTIVE: To clarify values regarding money.

- Divide the class into pairs. Read the instructions and the questions aloud, and make sure everyone understands.
- Explain that this is a "values clarification" or "thinking about money" activity. Tell students to talk about all the questions before they begin writing!
- After students finish writing, have them read their paragraphs to the class.
- *Variation:* Collect the paragraphs and read them to the class. (Or photocopy the paragraphs, omitting the name of the student being described, and distribute them randomly.) Have the class guess who the paragraph is about. Have the students agree or disagree with the original work. As students read the paragraphs, the "original" writer should identify him or herself.

Speech

- Read the instructions aloud. Brainstorm possibilities for things from the students' favorite store that they could bring to show the class. The store does not have to be local; it can be their favorite store in their countries. Model a very brief speech.
- Follow the suggested procedures on page T33.

EXPANSION

- For more review of vocabulary, show transparencies again and have students name as many vocabulary items as they can remember.

- •• For conversation review, have groups list questions about shopping that students can ask each other. Write the questions on the board, and have students practice them with partners.

- ••• Have students write a journal entry in the **Journal** section of their notebooks on "My Favorite Store."

UNIT TEST

- A **conversation test** and a **vocabulary test** for this unit are located in the back of this Teacher's Guide, plus suggestions for administration. Feel free to make as many copies as you need.

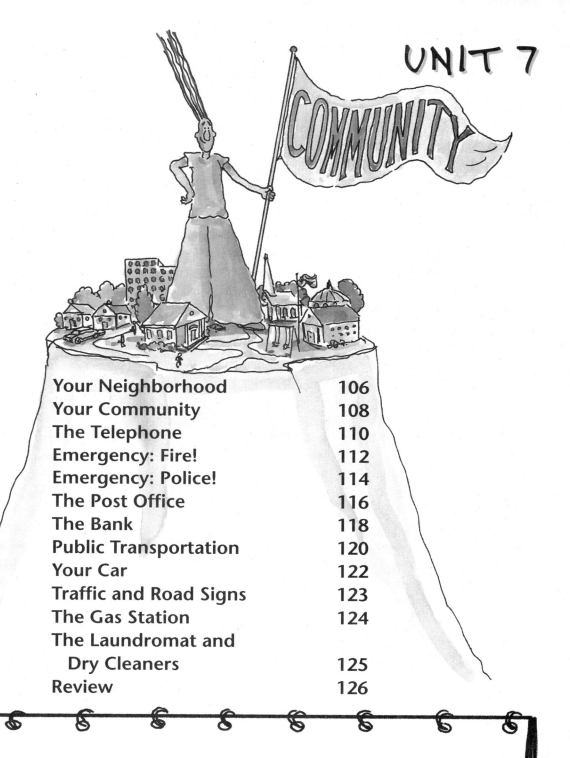

COMMUNITY

LEARNING STRATEGIES

➤ Walk around your neighborhood. Make a list of everything you see. Then, in the Journal section of your notebook, describe your neighborhood. What different kinds of houses did you see? Focus on two or three people that you saw. Describe them.

➤ Find places in your community where you can speak English. Go there. Introduce yourself. Speak English!

YOUR NEIGHBORHOOD

WARM UP

- Ask students what things are in their neighborhoods. Start by giving a few suggestions: houses? apartment buildings? streets? sidewalks? etc.
- Write YOUR NEIGHBORHOOD on the board. List the vocabulary on the board and have students copy the words into the **Vocabulary** section of their notebooks.

IN THE TEXT

- With the students, look at the illustrations on both pages of the text, or show the transparency with student books closed.
- To introduce the vocabulary, see the suggested procedures in **TO THE TEACHER**.
- Ask students how the illustration in their books is similar to and different from their neighborhoods. Help students describe the similarities and differences.

Class Discussion

- Follow the suggested procedures on page T29.

Find Someone Who

- Follow the suggested procedures on page T12.

EXPANSION

- Have students draw a rough sketch of their neighborhood, label everything in it, and explain their drawings to a partner. As an example, first draw your own neighborhood on the board and explain it.

•• Have students make lists of good and bad things in their neighborhoods. Have them read their lists to a small group of students and discuss the lists. Then make a master list on the board. Write headings: GOOD and BAD. Discuss the differences.

••• Have students describe differences and similarities between their neighborhood where they used to live and their neighborhood now.

YOUR COMMUNITY

WARM UP

- Bring to class a large city map or small copies of a local map, or draw a picture of the local area on the board. Also bring telephone directories. Use these as references throughout this topic.
- Write COMMUNITY on the board. Ask students if they know the names of any buildings or special places in the community. List on the board every place they name.
- Ask if they know where the buildings or special places are located. Have them explain where they are, or look up the addresses and locations in the telephone directories and on the maps.

IN THE TEXT

- To introduce the vocabulary, see the suggested procedures in **TO THE TEACHER**.
- Ask students questions about the map that will direct them to use direction/location vocabulary:

  What is next to the _____?
  Where is the_____?
  What is in front of _____? etc.

- Ask students if they know any other words for giving directions. If they do, have students add the words to the vocabulary box in the text.
- Practice these words and phrases using the map in the text. Then practice them again using the local maps. You may want to write sets of directions to important places in your community on the board and have students copy the directions in the **Community** section of their notebooks.

Class Discussion

- Follow the suggested procedures on page T29.

Partner Role Play

OBJECTIVE: To use maps and new vocabulary to ask for and give directions; to role play the conversations with a partner.

- Divide the class into pairs. Read the instructions and the partial conversations together. Make sure students understand they must complete *all* of the conversations. Circulate; help as needed.
- Have students practice the conversations. Then ask different pairs to present a conversation for the class; have each pair present only one role play.
- *Variation:* These role plays can be done as a puppet show. Make hand puppets with small paper bags, and use a table and sheet for a stage.

EXPANSION

- Do more partner role plays using the local maps. Have students ask for and give directions from the school to the local post office, the nearest bank, the nearest restaurant, the city hall, the hospital, the nearest gas station, the public library, the nearest police station, etc.

- ● Did any students in your class ever get lost in a new place? Have them tell their stories to the class. Encourage other students to ask questions. Ask a question if you need to get the "ball rolling."

THE TELEPHONE

WARM UP

- Bring in telephones—either telephone company phone sets that students can actually call each other on, or modular phones to use as props.
- Ask students if they know the parts of the telephone. Hold up a telephone and point to the receiver, cord, etc. If students can give you the vocabulary words, write them on the board.
- Ask students if they like to talk on the telephone. Ask who they talk to and what they like to talk about. Ask who doesn't like to talk on the telephone and why.

IN THE TEXT

- Look at the illustrations with the students, or show the transparency with books closed.
- To introduce the vocabulary, see the suggested procedures in **TO THE TEACHER**.
- Ask what is happening in each strip of pictures. Ask *Which is a directory assistance call? a wrong number? a long distance call? an answering machine call? a call "on hold"?*

Class Discussion

OBJECTIVE: To use new vocabulary to tell strip stories.

- With the class make up a story for each of the strip stories. Get started by asking

  Who are the people?
  Who or what are they calling?
  What are they saying?
  What are they hearing?
  What is happening?
  What is going to happen?

Partner Interview

- Follow the suggested procedures on page T4.

Cross-Cultural Exchange

OBJECTIVE: To compare telephoning procedures in different countries.

- Follow the suggested procedures on page T74.
- Have students give detailed explanations, including what you hear, what you say, what you do. How do public telephones work in different countries? Have students ever had a problem trying to use a telephone in a foreign country? Have them tell the story.

Partner Role Play

OBJECTIVE: To complete and role play a wrong number and an answering machine call.

- Divide the class into pairs. Tell the class that each pair must decide who is calling, who each call is for, and what each call is about.
- Read together the partial conversations from the page. Check for pronunciation. Explain what kinds of phrases need to fit into the missing parts and have students give suggestions, but don't write them down. Circulate as the students complete their telephone conversations and practice them; help as needed.
- When most pairs are finished, have different pairs read one conversation in front of the class. Or, if the class is large, divide into groups of three pairs and have each pair read their conversations to the group. Then have each group select one conversation from that group to be presented (with telephone props) to the whole class.

Partner Role Play

OBJECTIVE: To write and role play telephone conversations for everyday situations.

- This activity is more difficult than the preceding one. You may need to simplify it, either by assigning only one situation to each pair or by assigning it as a writing task for homework.
- Follow the suggested procedures on page T93, using the telephones as props.

Community Activity

OBJECTIVE: To find addresses and telephone numbers in a local telephone directory.

- Have students do this activity in pairs or groups of three. Use local telephone directories or pages copied from a directory.
- Together with the class, read the instructions and list of places to find in the directory. Explain that the first column of lines is for the names of the places. Look up the first one or two places together.
- While students are working, copy the chart on the board.
- When nearly everyone is done, have students report what they have found. Have one student copy the answers on the board.
- Have students write important information in the **Community** section of their notebooks.

EXPANSION

- Bring a telephone bill to class, or make a copy of the bill for each student. Read and discuss the bill together, noting local and long distance charges, service charges, tax, etc. If you pay for extra services, such as call waiting or special-rate discount packages, discuss these.
- • Ask students how much it costs to call home to their family or country for one minute. How often do they make international calls? How long do they talk? How much does it cost? What country codes do they use?

EMERGENCY: FIRE!

WARM UP

- Ask students what kinds of fires they have seen in the newspaper, on TV, in real life (house fires, hotel fires, forest fires, burning leaves, brush fires, car fires, etc.).
- If you can, show a video of a fire scene from a movie or the news.

IN THE TEXT

- Look at the illustration with the students, or show the transparency with books closed.
- To introduce the vocabulary, see the suggested procedures in **TO THE TEACHER**.
- Have the students tell you what kind of fire they see in the illustration, what is happening, and all the things they see. Write the vocabulary on the board.

Class Discussion

OBJECTIVE: To use new vocabulary to discuss causes and prevention of fires.

- Follow the suggested procedures on page T29.
- Take notes on this class discussion. Encourage students to take notes, too. Write two headings on the board: CAUSES OF FIRES and PREVENTION OF FIRES.
- Ask the class *How did this fire start?* Have students brainstorm as many possibilities as they can, and list them under CAUSES. Follow the same procedure with PREVENTION questions.
- Ask about other causes and preventions of fires. List them. Stress how to prevent fires at home.
- When the discussion is finished, recap the notes on the board orally, and ask students to summarize the discussion based on the notes.

What's the Story?
OBJECTIVE: To create a group story using a fire rescue situation and vocabulary.

- Follow the suggested procedures on page T23.
- Help the students choose who they write about, for example, an observer on the street, one of the victims, a firefighter, or an emergency medical technician.

Group Discussion
OBJECTIVE: To integrate new vocabulary into the context of students' experiences with fire.

- Explain that in this group discussion the student will interview all the members of his or her group.
- *Variation:* This activity can be structured as a **Partner Interview**.
- Practice reading the five questions together with the whole class. Make sure everyone understands all the questions.
- Divide the class into groups of two or four. Tell the students to take turns asking questions.
- When the students have completed their discussion, ask each group to choose the most interesting stories to tell to the whole class.

Partner Role Play
OBJECTIVE: To write and role play a telephone conversation to report a fire.

- Divide the class into pairs. Tell the class that each pair must decide on details of the fire: Where is it? How did it start? How bad is it?
- As the students write their telephone conversations. Circulate; help as needed.
- Have students decide who will be the *caller* and who will be the *911 operator*.
- Either have every pair read their conversation in front of the class, or divide into groups of four pairs and have each pair read their conversation to the group. Then each group can select one conversation to read to the whole class.

EXPANSION

- Have a fire department representative talk to the class about fire hazards.
- • Bring in fire-prevention flyers and discuss them.

EMERGENCY: POLICE!

WARM UP

- Bring in local newspapers from the past week or two. (If possible, use small town papers, not large city papers.) As students arrive, have them form groups and take newspapers and look in them for **Police Reports**. Read the Police Reports together.
- Write POLICE EMERGENCIES on the board. List the different kinds of problems that you read about in the Police Reports.
- Note that for this topic, the passive voice is commonly used. Since most of your students will probably not know passive voice, teach passive voice phrases as chunks on the board. Write the phrases or sentences: Car was stolen; he was mugged; house was broken into, etc.).
- Ask students if any of these things have ever happened to any of them, or to anyone they know. If any students say yes, have them tell the story to the class.

IN THE TEXT

- Look at the illustrations with the students, or show the transparency with books closed.
- Ask students what they see in the illustrations. Ask what is happening in each.
- To introduce the vocabulary, see the suggested procedures in **TO THE TEACHER**.

Strip Story

OBJECTIVE: To use new vocabulary to complete conversations in strip stories.

- Read the instructions with the class. Explain that the task is to make up partial conversations for each illustration.
- Have students divide informally into groups of three, and ask them to fill in all the bubbles with their groups.
- Ask each group to report their conversation for the first illustration; write the conversations on the board. Have the class discuss the options and decide as a whole which one is best for the situation. Do the same for the other illustrations.
- Tell the story together. Discuss the importance of understanding the commands of authorities in a foreign language and in a different culture.

Group Decision

OBJECTIVE: To discuss and decide what to do in emergency situations.

- Look at the emergency-situation illustrations together, and ask the students what is happening in each. Write new vocabulary on the board.
- Divide the class into groups of four.
- Have each group decide what they would do if they were in each of the situations pictured.
- Have each student in the group be responsible for recording and reporting on the group's decision for one of the four illustrations.
- Write the different decisions on the board, discuss them together, and decide as a class which are best.

Partner Activity

OBJECTIVE: To write and present a telephone conversation to report an emergency to the police.

- Divide the class into pairs. Have each pair choose one of the emergency situations pictured or make up another emergency situation.
- Tell them to make up answers to the six questions, and include them in a telephone conversation with a 911 operator.
- Have pairs decide who will be the *caller* and who will be the *911 operator*.
- Either have every pair read their conversation in front of the class, or combine pairs into groups of four and have each pair read their conversation to their group. Then each group can select one conversation to read to the whole class.

EXPANSION

- Have students in groups look through the newspapers to find news stories that are police emergencies. Read the stories to the class (or, if a story is long, summarize it) and discuss the stories.

- • Discuss local issues. Invite a police officer to talk to the class about safety precautions at home and on the street.

THE POST OFFICE

WARM UP

- Bring in as much realia as you can to teach this vocabulary: postcards, stamps, envelopes in different sizes, stationery, junk mail, a letter, an Express Mail envelope and label, a Priority Mail envelope and label.
- Hold up each item and ask students what it is. List the vocabulary on the board.
- Ask students *Where is the post office? What can you do at the post office?* List the actions on the board.
- Show your stationery again and ask students *What kind of paper do you write letters on?* Elicit as much vocabulary as you can, including sizes of paper, colors, lined/unlined, perfumed, decorations, and write it on the board.

IN THE TEXT

- To introduce the vocabulary, see the suggested procedures in **TO THE TEACHER**.
- Ask the students *What things do you see in the picture? Does this look like the post office you go to?* Elicit as much vocabulary as possible before looking at the vocabulary box.
- Explain some of the postal services, such as parcel post, first class, third class, overnight mail, insurance.

Class Discussion

OBJECTIVE: To use new vocabulary to describe post office activity.

- Explain that you will be taking notes on this class discussion. Encourage students to take notes, too.
- Write two headings on the board: CUSTOMERS and POST OFFICE EMPLOYEES. Ask what the customers are doing and what the post office employees are doing, and list their activities under each heading. Encourage the students to do likewise.

Class Game: *"What do you remember?"*

OBJECTIVE: To test observation and practice remembering detail.

- Read the instructions with the class. Tell students to look at the illustration and remember what is in it.
- Have them close their books and list everything they can remember about the illustration.
- Divide the class into groups of four. Have the groups compare notes and add to their lists. Have groups report what they remember about the illustration.
- Show the transparency of the illustration. Which group had the most detail? They are the winners!
- *Variation:* Have students report to the class individually.

Partner Activity

OBJECTIVE: To create a story about a post office situation with a partner.

- Divide the class into pairs. Read the instructions and the questions aloud together. Make sure the students understand that they must choose only one of the customers at the post office to tell about.
- Circulate; help as needed.
- When the stories are finished, have each pair read their story to the class.
- Ask the class to describe the stories. Which ones were funny? sad? exciting? romantic? happy? strange?

Partner Role Play

- Follow the suggested procedures on page T93.

Partner Interview

- Follow the suggested procedures on page T4.

Group Problem Posing/Problem Solving

OBJECTIVE: To include everyone in the decision-making process, and to use post office vocabulary in a discussion.

- Read the instructions aloud. Have the students state the problem in writing.
- Divide the class into groups of three. Tell students that everyone in the group must read their description of the problem to the group, and the group must decide on a solution together.
- Have groups report back to the class.

EXPANSION

- Bring in forms from the post office, discuss their purpose, and fill them out together.

THE BANK

WARM UP

- Bring in as much realia as you can: a checkbook, bank statement, deposit receipt, withdrawal receipt, savings deposit slip, etc. Hand them out at random to members of the class.
- Write BANK on the board. Ask students to look at the things you have given them and tell you what they are.
- Have them spell the words for you as you write them on the board.

IN THE TEXT

- Look at the illustration with the students, or show the transparency with books open or closed.
- To introduce the vocabulary, see the suggested procedures in **TO THE TEACHER**.

Class Activity

OBJECTIVE: **To describe bank activities.**

- Have students look at the illustration again and choose one person to describe. For example, *The woman at the counter is cashing a check, making a withdrawal, taking the cash from the teller.*
- Continue with the rest of the people in the illustration.
- Have one student come to the board and make a list of all of the activities.

Class Discussion

OBJECTIVE: **To integrate new vocabulary into the context of students' experiences; to listen to other students' experiences.**

- Write six headings on the board: CLOSEST BANK, USE BANK?, WHEN?, SAVINGS?, CHECKING?, SAFETY DEPOSIT BOX. As the students answer your questions, fill in columns with their answers under each heading.
- When the discussion is finished, orally recap the information on the board with the students.
- *Variation:* Have students divide informally into groups of three. In their groups have them ask and answer all the questions, then sit as a whole class and report as groups.

Group Problem Posing/Problem Solving

OBJECTIVE: To discuss problems at a bank, and to decide as a group what to do in each situation.

- Read the instructions aloud, look at the three bank problem illustrations, and discuss them with the class.
- Divide the class into groups of three. Have students figure out answers to all the questions and record their answers.
- Have each group select a *reporter* to report the answers to the class.
- Compare different groups' solutions, and have the class decide which answers are best.
- Have the class decide which groups they would like to see role play each of the three situations. Have the groups present the role plays without scripts.

EXPANSION

- "20 Questions" Game: *What is in my safety deposit box?* You be the first leader. Use one of the items from the safety deposit box list (from **Class Discussion** question 5, page 118) on the board (or if that list is too short, use other vocabulary from the text). Decide what you would keep in a safety deposit box. Have students guess colors, sizes, price, etc. They have twenty questions to guess the item. The one who guesses becomes the next leader.

- • With the class, write five or six questions for a **Find Someone Who** activity (has a checking account, would like to work in a bank, likes to save money, doesn't like to go to a bank, etc). List the questions on the board. Have students copy the questions into the **Activities** section of their notebooks. Have them follow the suggested procedures for **Find Someone Who** on page T12.

- ••• Discuss similarities and differences between banks in different countries the members of your class have lived in. Are security measures different? Is the technology different? Is there a black market for changing money? How does it work? etc.

PUBLIC TRANSPORTATION

WARM UP

- Write PUBLIC TRANSPORTATION on the board. Ask the students what it means. Have them give examples of public transportation, and list the examples on the board.
- Ask the students what transportation they use to come to school. Write this list on the board. Ask them how many of the kinds of transportation on this list are "public transportation."
- Ask how many students in the class use public transportation. How many have used public transportation in other countries?

IN THE TEXT

- Look at the illustrations with the students, or show the transparency with books closed.
- To introduce the vocabulary, see the suggested procedures in **TO THE TEACHER**.
- Ask the students what they see in the illustration. Point to details in the illustration and ask *What is happening here? What is this man/woman doing?*

Class Discussion

OBJECTIVE: **To integrate new vocabulary into the context of students' experiences; to listen to other students' experiences and take notes.**

- Follow the suggested procedures on page T29.
- Take notes on this class discussion. Encourage students to take notes, too. Assign one student to write the notes on the board.
- As you ask the class questions and students answer, have the student at the board write the number of the question and add appropriate notes beside the number. (For example: 1: bus, taxi, train.)
- When the discussion is finished, recap the notes on the board orally with the students.

Group Role Play

- Follow the suggested procedures on page T69.

Group Problem Posing/Problem Solving

OBJECTIVE: To discuss common public transportation problems with a group, and to decide together how to solve them.

- Read the instructions aloud. Read each of the three problems with the class, and make sure students understand each problem.
- Have students write possible solutions for all three problems in the **Activities** section of their notebooks.
- Divide the class into groups of three. Tell the students to read their possible solutions to their groups. Then have the groups decide which solutions they like best.
- Ask groups to choose a *reporter* to tell the class about the group's decisions. After all groups have reported, discuss all the possibilities with the class and decide which solutions the whole class prefers.

Group Survey

- Follow the suggested procedures on page T19.

EXPANSION

- Have small groups choose one of the people in the public transportation illustration to write a story about. Follow the suggested procedures for **What's the Story?** on page T23.

YOUR CAR

WARM UP

- Bring in as many pictures of cars, as you can, and ask students to bring in car pictures. They can be from magazines, cereal boxes, newspapers, posters, photographs, etc.
- Divide the class into as many groups as there are pictures. Have each group make a list of things that describe their car, and choose a *reporter* to describe their car to the class.
- Ask students *Who likes to drive?* and *Where do you like to drive?* How many students have ever been in a car accident? What happened? Who was driving? Have them tell their stories to the class (or to a group, if the class is very large).

IN THE TEXT

- Look at the illustration with the students or show the transparency with books closed.
- To introduce the vocabulary, see the suggested procedures in **TO THE TEACHER**.
- Point to parts of the car illustration and say *What part is this?*

Partner Interview

- Follow the suggested procedures on page T4.

EXPANSION

- ••• Divide the class into partners to look at the illustration of the car and discuss it. Then have students close their books. Have partners list everything they can remember together about the car. Pair partner groups into groups of four. Have the groups compare notes and add to their lists. Have groups report what they remember to the class.

TRAFFIC AND ROAD SIGNS

WARM UP

- Draw the shapes of these signs on the board: STOP, YIELD, and RAILROAD CROSSING. Have the students guess what signs these shapes could represent. Ask the students if they know any other shapes of signs.

IN THE TEXT

- Have students look at the signs together—or at the transparency—and guess what each sign means.
- Alternatively, divide students into groups of four. Have each group make a list of the meanings of the 17 signs on the page and report their list to the class.
- List on the board the name of each sign: *STOP, YIELD, DO NOT ENTER, SCHOOL CROSSING, SCHOOL, PEDESTRIAN CROSSING, NO U TURN, NO LEFT TURN, NO RIGHT TURN, NO TRUCKS OVER 4 TONS ALLOWED, NO BICYCLES ALLOWED, PUBLIC TELEPHONE, ONE WAY TRAFFIC (TO THE RIGHT ONLY), ROAD SLIPPERY WHEN WET, STEEP INCLINE ON HILL, SPEED LIMIT 55, RAILROAD CROSSING.*
- Have students copy the list in the **Vocabulary** section of their notebooks.

Class Discussion

OBJECTIVE: **To become familiar with traffic and road signs.**

- Follow the suggested procedures on page T29.
- Ask students what the traffic and road signs look like in their countries. What colors and shapes are they? What pictures are on them? What words? Have students draw signs on the board to demonstrate.

Community Activity

OBJECTIVE: **To become familiar with the traffic and road signs in your community and to understand their meanings.**

- Ask students which of these signs are in their community and where they are located.
- Discuss the colors of signs and their meanings: red/yellow for warning, green for highway information, brown for tourist information, etc.
- For homework have students draw the signs in their neighborhoods, including the colors.
- In the next class, divide the class into groups of four students, and have the students show and explain their drawings to each other.
- Discuss the drawings as a class. Are there any signs that everyone had? any that only some students noticed? any that are in their community but not in the illustration?

EXPANSION

- Ask students how to get a license in their state. Ask how to register a car and buy insurance. Ask how much insurance costs where they live. Write the answers on the board.

- •• Use any word or phrase from the unit. For example, **brake**. The next student in the chain has to think of a word beginning with **e**, such as **engine**. The next student thinks of a word beginning with **e**. Continue around the room. Write any new vocabulary words on the board. Have students copy the new words into the **Vocabulary** section of their notebooks.

THE GAS STATION

WARM UP

- What kinds of things do people buy and do at a gas station? Ask students to make a list on the board.
- Ask students how much gas costs where they live. Is it more or less expensive here than in their home country? Compare gasoline prices in different places.

IN THE TEXT

- To introduce the vocabulary, see the suggested procedures in **TO THE TEACHER**.
- Ask *What does "self service" mean? "full service"? Which do you prefer?* Talk about **gallon, lever, lift.**

Partner Activity

OBJECTIVE: To write and role play a conversation to ask for assistance for a car.

- Divide the class into pairs. Tell the class that each pair must decide what to say in all four situations, and write a conversation between a car owner and someone who can help—a service station attendant or mechanic, another motorist, etc.
- Read together the situations from the page. Check for comprehension. Ask who the two people in the conversation might be in each situation; write possibilities on the board.
- As the students write their conversations and practice them, circulate; help as needed.
- When most are finished, either have every pair read their conversation in front of the class, or, if the class is large, divide the class into groups of four and have each pair read their conversation to their group.
- Have each group select one conversation to be read to the whole class.

Group Vocabulary Challenge

- Follow the suggested procedures on page T17.

EXPANSION

- Make a list with the class of things to do for regular car maintenance (change the oil, check the air pressure in the tires, etc.).
- •• Have partners list all the car repairs they can think of and read their lists to the class. Which pair had the longest list?

THE LAUNDROMAT AND DRY CLEANERS

WARM UP

- Bring in as much realia as you can to teach this vocabulary and to use for the pantomime and role play activities. (Bring laundry detergent, spot spray, bleach, and clothing and towels of different fabrics and colors.)
- Have students volunteer to come to the front of the class, choose an item, and explain what it is. List the vocabulary on the board.
- Write LAUNDROMAT and DRY CLEANERS on the board. Ask students what can be washed at the laundromat and what needs to be dry cleaned. List answers and discuss differences of opinion.

IN THE TEXT

- Look at the illustration in the text, or show the transparency with books closed.
- To introduce the vocabulary, see the suggested procedures in **TO THE TEACHER**.
- Ask students what is happening in the illustration. What are the people doing?

Partner Game: *"What do you remember?"*
OBJECTIVE: To test observation and practice remembering detail.

- Divide the class into pairs.
- Have each pair look at the illustration and discuss it, then close their texts and together list everything they can remember.
- Combine partner groups into groups of four. Have the groups compare notes, add to their lists, and read them to the class. Show the transparency of the illustration or have students open their texts and look at the illustration. Which group had the longest list?

What's the Story?

- Follow the suggested procedures on page T23.

EXPANSION

- Role play the stories created above, using the realia from the **WARM UP** as props.
- •• Have one student volunteer to pantomime using the realia from the **WARM UP**. Have the rest of the class give him or her instructions for sorting, washing, drying, and folding clothes. Help structure the instructions by writing headings on the board: SORT WASH DRY FOLD. List more detailed instructions as students give them (separate light and dark clothes, etc.).

REVIEW

IN THE TEXT

Speech

OBJECTIVE: To reinforce important community and neighborhood vocabulary by using it in an informal presentation to the class.

- Follow the suggested procedures on page T33.

Partner Vocabulary Challenge

OBJECTIVE: To review vocabulary for the entire unit.

- Divide the class into pairs. Set a time limit, such as 5 minutes, for each of the five questions.
- Tell the students not to look at other pages of the text or in a dictionary.
- Have the pairs write the bank list first, then compare lists with another pair. Write a master list on the board, and have everyone copy the words into the **Vocabulary** section of their notebooks.
- Follow the same procedure with the other four questions.

Community Activity

OBJECTIVE: To review giving directions from a personal map.

- Have each student draw a map from the school to his or her house. (This may be a homework assignment.)
- Have different students explain their maps to the class.
- *Variation:* Divide the class into pairs, and have them explain their drawings to each other. Combine pairs into groups of four students. Have partners explain each other's directions (*not their own!*) to the other two students in the group. Afterward, ask if they had any problems and why.

EXPANSION

- For more review of vocabulary, show the transparencies again with student books closed, and then have students name as many vocabulary items as they can remember.

- •• For conversation review, have groups list questions about shopping that students can ask each other. Write the questions on the board, and have students practice them with partners.

UNIT TEST

- A **conversation test** and a **vocabulary test** for this unit are located in the back of this Teacher's Guide, plus suggestions for administration. Feel free to make as many copies as you need.

WORK

LEARNING STRATEGIES

➤ Make a list in English every day of work to do in your home.

➤ With a friend from class, make a list of jobs and work situations in your community that require English.

WORK EVERYBODY DOES!

WARM UP

- Ask students about housework. What kind of tasks do they do around the home?
- Write LIKE and HATE on the board.
- Ask students which tasks they hate and which they like, if any. Have one student come to the board and list all of the tasks students hate. Another student can list the tasks students like.

IN THE TEXT

- Look at the illustrations on both pages of the text, or show the transparencies with books closed.
- Ask students what they see in the illustrations, and list all the vocabulary on the board. Ask them if they like to do each of these jobs.
- Review other pages where some of the vocabulary words are presented (for example, page 20).
- Write the heading THINGS WE USE on the board. Ask students what things we use to do each of the jobs in the illustrations. List all the items shown in the illustrations (*iron, furniture polish, dust cloth, dish towel, sponge*, etc.), and have students copy them into the **Vocabulary** section of their notebooks.

Group Survey

- Follow the suggested procedures on page T19.

Class Game: *"Test your memory"*

OBJECTIVE: To listen to a story and match illustrations with words; to put events in correct sequence.

- Have students describe the illustrations on page 129. Write any new vocabulary on the board.
- Have the students give names to each of the family members.
- Read the story to the class and have students listen, with books closed.

> *It's Saturday morning, and the Diego family is very busy at home. Carmen is folding the wash. Her husband, Ramon, is defrosting the freezer. Their daughter, Teresa, is raking the leaves. Their son, Tomas, is hammering a nail into the wall to hang a picture. After lunch, Carmen's mother, Mrs. Rivera, begins cooking dinner. Carmen is dusting the furniture, and Ramon is washing the windows. After washing the windows, Ramon changes a light bulb. Then he feeds the dog. All the housework is done, and it's finally time for dinner.*

- Read the story again, this time with students looking at the illustrations in the book. Have students number each illustration as you read the story.
- When the story is complete, have the students describe it back to you in the correct order.

Cross-Cultural Exchange

OBJECTIVE: To compare housework customs and traditions in different cultures.

- This activity can be done as a partner interview, as a small group activity, or as a whole class discussion. If you are working with partners or groups, combine cultures and sexes in each pair or group for a lively discussion.
- Follow the suggested procedures on page T74.

EXPANSION

- With the class, brainstorm ten questions about housework. Write the questions on the board as the class poses them. Either divide the class into pairs and use the questions for a **Partner Interview**, or use the questions for a **Find Someone Who** class activity.
- •• Pantomime some kind of work around the house and ask the students what you are doing. When a student guesses, have the student come to the front of the class and pantomime another kind of household job.
- ••• Have students make lists of hard work and easy work at home. Have them read and discuss their lists in small groups. Then have the whole class make a master list on the board of HARD WORK and EASY WORK. Discuss differences of opinion.

HOME REPAIRS

WARM UP

- Ask students to bring in something they use to do home repairs. Bring in some things yourself and explain to the class what you do with them. Have students explain their items. Write new vocabulary on the board.
- Review vocabulary of related units, such as on page 78.

IN THE TEXT

- Look at the illustrations with the students, or show the transparency with books closed.
- To introduce the vocabulary, see the suggested procedures in **TO THE TEACHER**.

Class Activity

OBJECTIVE: To associate vocabulary for tools with corresponding vocabulary for work.

- Write two headings on the board: TOOLS and WORK.
- Ask for a student volunteer to record vocabulary on the board.
- Have students name a tool and then the work you can do with that tool.
- As the student records words on the board, have the class help with spelling. (If your class is familiar with much of the vocabulary for tools, have students close their books for this activity; otherwise, use the books for assistance.)

Group Decision

OBJECTIVE: To use new vocabulary in a group to find solutions to problems at home.

- Practice reading the five problems together with the whole class. Make sure everyone understands all the problems.
- Divide the class into groups of five. Have each group choose a *recorder* to write down the group's solution to each problem. Circulate; help as needed.
- Have each recorder write the group's solutions on the board and read them to the class. Discuss the solutions. Are they the same? different? Which solutions does everyone prefer? Why?

What's the Story?

- Have students look at the illustrations on page 130.
- Follow the suggested procedures on page T23.

Find Someone Who

- Follow the suggested procedures on page T12.

EXPANSION

- With the class, make up yes/no questions for home repairs that can be used for a **Find Someone Who** activity (*Do you have a screwdriver at home? Did you ever fix a leaky faucet? Did you ever fix a broken window? Do you have a saw at home?* etc.) Follow the procedures for **Find Someone Who** on page T12.

- •• Write on the board *What kinds of sewing do you do?* Underneath, write two headings: MAKE THINGS and MEND THINGS. Ask students *What things do you make? What things do you mend?* From their answers, write lists of things to make and things to mend on the board. Review the lists together, drawing conclusions about the kinds of sewing done by students in the class. If students have made clothing or other things, have them show the class their handiwork and tell the class about it.

JOBS

WARM UP

- Bring in pictures from magazines and newspapers showing different jobs. Show them to the students and see how many jobs they can name. Write JOBS on the board, and list all the jobs they name.
- Ask students what their jobs are now and what jobs they had in the past. If they mention jobs not on the list, add them to the list on the board.
- Ask students about their parents' jobs. Ask about other family members. Are there any family businesses or family occupations in the class?
- If all students are in school or not working, ask what jobs students would like to have in the future.
- Point out present, past, and future tense.
- Have students copy the new vocabulary into the **Vocabulary** section of their notebooks.

IN THE TEXT

- Look at the illustrations on both pages of the text, or show the transparency with books closed.
- To introduce the vocabulary, see the suggested procedures in **TO THE TEACHER**.
- Ask students what jobs these people have. Review some jobs that are presented on other pages, such as *teacher* (page 14).

Class Discussion

OBJECTIVE: To integrate new vocabulary into the context of students' experiences.

- Ask students where each person in the illustration works and what he or she does.
- Ask students what jobs appeal to them. Which look like fun? Which one looks hardest? Which looks easiest?

Group Activity

OBJECTIVE: To correlate vocabulary for job titles, job descriptions, and job locations.

- Divide the class into groups of five students. Read the instructions and the chart together, and make sure everyone understands all the vocabulary. Write on the board *What does a farm worker do? Where does a farm worker work?* Explain that students must answer these questions for every job. Circulate; help as needed.
- Have each group select a *reporter* to read the group's chart to the class. If there are differences in any group's answers, discuss the differences.

Group Activity

OBJECTIVE: To describe jobs with a group, decide together on a desirable job, and describe it.

- Before starting, have students look at the four illustrations. Ask questions about the jobs shown. Help with any new vocabulary, and have students copy any new words into the **Vocabulary** section of their notebooks.
- Have the class remain in their groups of five. Read the instructions together and explain that students need to label each of the illustrations, make their own picture, and label it. When the groups are finished, have them report their decisions to the class. Did any groups choose similar jobs? Did groups have any trouble agreeing on a job? If so, what was the disagreement?

Partner Role Play

OBJECTIVE: To write and role play a TV interview about a job.

- Divide the class into pairs. Tell the class that each pair must decide on a job for the interview. Tell them the class is presenting a TV special on jobs, and each pair will do an interview on a different job. Make sure the students do not select the same jobs.
- Bring a prop to class for each of the jobs: a construction hat, a nurse's cap, etc., or encourage students to make simple paper props for their interviews.
- Read the sample questions from the page together. Check for pronunciation.
- Ask for or suggest sample answers to each question.
- Have students decide who will be the *TV host* and who will be the *worker*.
- As the students write their interviews and practice them, circulate; help as needed.
- When most are finished, either have every pair role play their interview in front of the class or, if the class is large, divide into groups of four pairs and have each pair read their interview to their own group. Have each group select one interview to be read to the whole class.
- *Variation:* Use a puppet show format.

EXPANSION

- Have students make individual lists of good jobs and bad jobs. Have them read their lists to a small group of students and compare the lists. Then have the whole class make a master list on the board of GOOD JOBS and BAD JOBS. Discuss differences of opinion.

- •• Have groups of students decide on a job and write clues about the job. Have them read their clues to the class, and have the class guess the job.

CLOTHING FOR WORK

WARM UP

- Bring to class articles of special work clothing or part of a uniform. Ask the students who would wear it.
- Write CLOTHING FOR WORK on the board.
- Ask students what clothing they wear to work. List the vocabulary on the board.
- Ask what jobs require special clothing, and list the answers on the board.

IN THE TEXT

- To introduce the vocabulary, see the suggested procedures in **TO THE TEACHER**.
- Ask students what jobs the people in the illustration have, and list all the answers on the board. Have the students tell you how to spell the words.
- Ask what the people are wearing. Elicit as much vocabulary as possible from the students.

Class Discussion

OBJECTIVE: To increase familiarity with special clothing for jobs, and take notes.

- Follow the suggested procedures on page T29.
- Take notes on this class discussion, and encourage students to take notes, too. Write eight headings on the board: WORK?, WHY SPECIAL CLOTHES?, WHO PAYS?, LIKE?, WHY?, SHOES?, HATS?, GLOVES? As you ask the class questions and the students answer, fill in columns under each heading with their answers. Have the students do likewise.
- When the discussion is finished, orally recap the notes on the board and ask individual students to summarize each line based on the notes.

Group Discussion

OBJECTIVE: To use new vocabulary to discuss appropriate clothing for work.

- Read the questions with the class; make sure everyone understands the four questions.
- Divide the students into groups of four; have them ask and answer all the questions in their groups.
- Have a *reporter* from each group read the answers to the questions to the class. If there is disagreement about what jobs the people have or whether their clothing is appropriate, discuss the assumptions and expectations behind their conclusions; there may be many possible answers to these questions, and the class may or may not agree in the end.
- At the end of the discussion, draw conclusions together. Your only conclusion to question 3 and question 4 may be: "It depends."

Cross-Cultural Exchange

OBJECTIVE: To compare work clothes in different countries.

- Follow the suggested procedures on page T74.

EXPANSION

- If any student has a uniform or other special work clothing at home, ask the student to wear/bring it to class and explain both the clothing and the job.

- •• Have students work in small groups and choose one of the people to write a story about. Give him or her a name. Describe a typical day. Follow the procedures for **What's the Story?** on page T23.

SAFETY AT WORK

WARM UP

- Ask students *Did you ever get hurt on the job? Do you know anyone who got hurt at work? What happened?*
- Ask students *What jobs are dangerous?* Make a list on the board of dangerous jobs. Then ask about each dangerous job: *What dangers are there on this job?* List the dangers next to each job. Finally, ask *What protection can you use?* Write the protection next to each danger.

IN THE TEXT

- Look at the illustration with the students, or show the transparency with books closed.
- To introduce the vocabulary, see the suggested procedures in **TO THE TEACHER**.

Class Discussion

OBJECTIVE: To integrate new vocabulary into the context of students' experiences; to listen to other students' experiences and take notes.

- Follow the suggested procedures on page T29.

Group Decision

OBJECTIVE: To use new vocabulary to create conversation for the safety violations illustration.

- Divide the class into groups of five.
- Tell the students to write conversations in the balloons to match the illustration. Circulate; help as needed.
- Have groups read their balloon captions to the class. Are they similar? What are the differences?

Class Discussion

OBJECTIVE: To discuss vocabulary of safety signs at work.

- Explain that you will be taking notes on this class discussion. Encourage students to take notes, too.
- Write three headings on the board: SIGNS, MEANING, and LOCATION. As you ask questions about each sign and students answer, fill in columns with their answers under each heading. Encourage the students to do likewise.
- When the discussion is finished, orally recap the notes on the board for the students, and ask students to summarize the discussion based on their notes.

Group Role Play

OBJECTIVE: To make group decisions, write a group conversation at work, and combine verbal and non-verbal simulation practice.

- Read the instructions for each role play, and have the class make suggestions for each. For role play 1, ask what job might several of them do, and what they are supposed to do on the job. For role play 2, ask what kinds of things people talk about when they are on a break.
- Divide the class into groups of four or five students. Have each group decide which situation to choose.
- Have each group write a script for the role play that includes a role for each student. Circulate; help as needed.
- Have students practice the role play, then present it to the class.

Community Activity

OBJECTIVE: To become familiar with signs at work, at school, and in the community.

- Ask students if they remember any signs at the school and what is on the signs. List them on the board.
- Divide the class into groups of three. Direct each group to a particular place in the school to look for signs. Give groups a time limit in which to find signs, copy any words they find on the signs, and come back to the classroom.
- Have each group copy their sign information on the board, then discuss the vocabulary and purpose of each sign.
- As homework, have students copy the words from signs at work and/or in the community. In the next class, have them write the signs on the board, then discuss them with the class.

EXPANSION

- Have pairs of students draw a safety sign. Then have students pantomime the action it represents, and have the class try to guess which action they are pantomiming. Show the class the sign so they can see if they are right or wrong.

WORKING ON A FARM

WARM UP

- Write ON A FARM on the board. Underneath write two headings: ANIMALS and WORK.
- Ask students what animals live on farms. Elicit as much vocabulary as possible, and write the animal types on the board.
- Ask students what work people do on farms, and again write their answers on the board.

IN THE TEXT

- To introduce the vocabulary, see the suggested procedures in **TO THE TEACHER**.
- The animal vocabulary can be fun as a bilingual or multilingual activity, with students comparing the vocabulary for mother, father, and baby animals in different languages.

Cross-Cultural Exchange

OBJECTIVE: To compare the rendering of animal sounds in different languages.

- Explain that animals "say" different things in different languages. Read the chart aloud to show the class what animals "say" in English.
- Ask students from every other language that may be represented in the class to tell what these animals "say" in their language. Have them write the words on the board in their language and pronounce them for the class. (Students may fill in the chart with their own language or with words from other students' languages, if that is more fun for them.)

IN THE TEXT

- Keep the texts open for this additional picture dictionary vocabulary activity, or show the transparency.
- To introduce the vocabulary, see the suggested procedures in **TO THE TEACHER**.

Class Discussion

OBJECTIVE: To integrate new farm vocabulary into a discussion of farm work.

- Explain that you will be taking notes on this class discussion. Encourage students to take notes, too.
- Write two headings on the board: FARM WORKERS and ACTIVITIES. Ask what the farm worker is doing in each illustration, and list his/her activities under each heading. Encourage the students to do likewise.
- Ask what other things are done on farms and ranches. Add to the lists.

Find Someone Who

- Follow the suggested procedures on page T12.

EXPANSION

- Bring in illustrations of farms and ranches from magazines or calendars. Divide the class into small groups, and pass out one illustration to each group. Have each member of the group write one sentence about the illustration on a piece of paper, fold it, and hand it to the next group member. When the last person finishes his/her sentence, he/she opens the folded paper and reads all of the group's sentences. Compare the groups' descriptions.

- •• Have students describe differences and similarities between farms they know about and the farms in the illustrations. Are they smaller? larger? Do they have the same animals? different ones? What crops do they raise? etc.

PROBLEMS AT WORK

WARM UP

- Write PROBLEMS AT WORK on the board. Underneath list:

  with the boss:
  with other employees:
  with other people:
  with equipment:
  with regulations:
  other:

- Ask students what kinds of problems people have with each. Write their answers in the spaces next to the list on the board. Elicit as much vocabulary as you can before opening the text.

IN THE TEXT

- Look at the illustrated problems on both pages of the text, or show the transparency with books closed.
- To introduce the vocabulary, see the suggested procedures in **TO THE TEACHER**.

Class Discussion

OBJECTIVE: To use new vocabulary to discuss problems at work.

- Have the students look at each illustration carefully. Ask them how the people in each illustration feel, and why. Ask if they know anyone who has ever experienced any of these problems. How did they feel at the time? What did they do? Does the class have any strong opinions about any of these problems?
- In the harassment picture, be sure to ask if students know what resources are available to them for issuing a complaint.

Group Problem Posing/Problem Solving

OBJECTIVE: To include everyone in the decision-making process, and use work-problem vocabulary in a discussion.

- Divide the class into groups of four. Tell students that everyone in the group must state at least one of the problems, and the group must choose one problem and together decide on a solution to it.
- Circulate; help as needed.
- When groups have finished, have each report their problem statement first.
- Have the class choose the best way to write their problem statements on the board.
- Then have each group role play its solution to a problem.
- Discuss the solutions with the class.
- Which solutions did the class like best? Why?

Conversation Squares

- Follow the suggested procedures on page T33.

EXPANSION

- Ask students if they can identify other problems at work (i.e., music, loud talking, smoking, bringing children to work, uncleanliness, messiness, bad language, etc.). On the board list the problems they mention. Discuss each problem, and give students information about appeals, resources, and their rights in each situation.

- • Make up five yes/no questions with the class about problems at work. *Did you ever have a problem at work? Did you ever have a lazy co-worker? Were you ever sexually harassed?* etc. Follow the suggested procedures for **Find Someone Who** on page T12.

LOSING YOUR JOB

WARM UP

- Write LOSING YOUR JOB on the board. Underneath write the heading REASONS.
- Ask students why people lose their jobs. List answers under REASONS.
- Ask why people *quit* their jobs.
- Have students copy any new vocabulary into the **Vocabulary** section of their notebooks.

IN THE TEXT

- Look at the illustrations on both pages of the text, or show the transparency with books closed.
- To introduce the vocabulary, see the suggested procedures in **TO THE TEACHER**.
- Ask students if any of the strip stories show reasons for leaving a job that are listed on the board. If any strip stories show reasons not listed, ask students what they think those reasons might be.

Strip Stories

OBJECTIVE: To use new vocabulary to write captions for strip stories about losing a job.

- Divide the class into pairs. Read the instructions together. Tell the students to make up a detailed story for each of the strip stories on both pages.
- *Variation*: Assign only one strip story to each pair.
- Put these questions on the board and tell students to answer them in their story: *Where is this company/farm? What is its name? How many people work there? What are their names? How long have they worked there? Why are they losing their jobs? What will they do now?*
- Circulate; help as needed.
- When most are finished, have a *reporter* from each pair tell their best story to the class.
- *Variation:* Combine pairs and have each pair tell all their stories to the other pair. If any of the stories are very similar or very different, tell the class why.

Find Someone Who

- Follow the suggested procedures on page T12.
- Review the present perfect tense for formation of *Have you ever. . .* questions.
- Refer to the **Grammar for Conversation** section in the back of the student text for examples of the present perfect tense.

Group Activity

OBJECTIVE: To integrate new vocabulary into the context of students' work experiences.

- Read the instructions and the three questions with the class; make sure everyone understands all the questions.
- Divide the class into groups of three, and tell them to ask and answer all the questions in their groups. Tell students to list as many *good* reasons as they can think of for each question.
- While students are working, write three headings on the board: REASONS TO QUIT, REASONS TO STAY, REASONS TO FIRE EMPLOYEE.
- When groups are finished, choose a group to write their list of good reasons to quit on the board, another group to write their good reasons to stay, and a third group to write their good reasons to fire an employee.
- Have the groups read their lists to the class, and ask if other groups have any other good reasons. Add them to the lists.
- Talk about the lists. Does everyone agree that all of the reasons are good reasons? If not, why not?
- When the discussion is finished, recap from the lists on the board and have students summarize the conclusions.

EXPANSION

- Have the same groups make lists of bad reasons to quit a job, to keep a job, and to fire an employee. Then have the whole class make a master list on the board of BAD REASONS. Discuss differences of opinion.

- •• Have the whole class participate in writing a skit for one or more of the strip stories on these two pages. Decide how many characters to include. Write both conversations and actions on the board. Have students volunteer to role play the skit for the class.

FINDING A JOB

WARM UP

- Bring in classified ads from a variety of sources: newspapers, postings, listings of jobs from bulletin boards, flyers, etc.
- Show the ads to the students and describe them (*This is a newspaper ad. This is a posting,* etc.). Ask students if they ever saw any ads like this, and where they saw them.
- Ask students how they look for jobs. List the ways.
- Ask how people get jobs in different countries.

IN THE TEXT

- Look at the illustration of the ads with the students, or show the transparency with books closed.
- Have students ask about any words or abbreviations they don't know; then discuss.
- Ask students questions about the ads: *What qualifications are important for a housekeeper? for a courier? for a counter position at Day Time Dry Cleaners? How can you apply for the security officer position? the courier job?* etc.
- Ask students how much they think these jobs would pay in their area. Ask how much the jobs would pay in other countries.

Class Discussion

OBJECTIVE: To integrate new vocabulary from classified ads into the context of students' experiences.

- Follow the suggested procedures on page T29.
- Question 4 may elicit a variety of inappropriate answers (*When it looks interesting; when I have time,* etc.). Write some of the answers on the board. Ask Question 5, and list answers on the board (*interesting work; I'm qualified*; etc.)
- Discuss efficient ways to look for a job.

Write

OBJECTIVE: To fill out a basic employment application.

- This is a simplified application. Go over each item with the students.
- Use the transparency and fill in a model application.
- Write any relevant vocabulary on the board for students to copy into the **Vocabulary** section of their notebooks.
- Have the students fill out the application themselves. Circulate; help as needed.
- When students finish, discuss and answer any questions.

Partner Role Play

OBJECTIVE: To write and role play a job interview.

- Explain that this will be a role play of a job interview. Together read the sample questions from the page. Check for pronunciation.
- Discuss appropriate dress and hairstyle for interviews and jobs, and appropriate body language (handshake, look interviewer in the eye, don't look down, etc.).
- Have a model role play, with a student and yourself using the questions and generating others, depending upon the job and the application.
- With the students, choose a job from the ad page and decide who will be the *interviewer*, who the *applicant*. (You, as teacher, should take one role to serve as a model.)
- Write relevant vocabulary on the board for students to copy into the **Vocabulary** section of their notebooks. Go through the interview. Have students make notes of any questions they have.
- Answer any questions from students about the interviews.
- Divide the class into pairs, and have them practice interviews, using the ads in the book and the applications. Have pairs switch roles.
- Ask several pairs to present their interviews for the class.

EXPANSION

- What jobs do the students currently have? Make a list on the board; then ask for a job description. Use your discretion in asking for a salary range for these jobs; it may not be an appropriate topic for your class. Discuss with students where they can get these jobs, what is available in students' vicinities, what they can expect about the jobs, etc.

- • What jobs would students like to have? Make another list, similar to the one above, with the same categories. You should come up with a useful document that students can use to find/improve/change their jobs. (You may need to do some research about addresses, phone numbers, and contact people.)

BENEFITS

WARM UP

- Ask students what job benefits they know about. Help them with the vocabulary, and write the benefits they mention on the board.

IN THE TEXT

- Look at the pictures in the text of people using job benefits, or show the transparency with books closed.
- To introduce the vocabulary, see the suggested procedures in **TO THE TEACHER**.

Class Discussion

OBJECTIVE: To clarify values regarding job benefits.

- Read the discussion questions with the class; make sure everyone understands both questions.
- Tell the students to number the different benefits *in order of their importance*, starting with 1 for the most important.
- While students are numbering, list the benefits on the board.
- Have students choose one or two partners to share and compare their value scales with.
- Have everyone sit as a whole class again. Ask how many students had trouble deciding which benefits were most important to them, and discuss why.
- Point to each of the benefits on the board and ask if anyone rated it 1. Write the number of students who say yes in each case. Discuss reasons for different choices, and draw conclusions together about the values of job benefits.

Group Discussion

OBJECTIVE: To integrate new vocabulary into the context of students' experiences; to listen and take notes.

- Practice reading the seven questions together with the whole class. Make sure everyone understands and can pronounce all the words.
- If some students do not have jobs, tell them to answer what they would like for job benefits. Give sample answers.
- Divide into groups of five or six. Students may divide the questions, or each one can ask the complete set of questions to a different student. When the discussion is finished, have students summarize their interviews based on their notes, and report as a group to the class.
- *Variation*: This activity can be structured as a **Partner Interview**.

Group Vocabulary Challenge

OBJECTIVE: To review vocabulary with a group.

- Keep the same groups and have each group choose a *recorder*.
- Ask each group to list, in five minutes, as many reasons to take a sick day as they can in the **Activities** section of their notebooks.
- When five minutes are up, have each group read back their list. Write the words on the board, correcting for spelling and whatever grammar may be used.

Class Game: *"What do you want to do on your next vacation?"*

- Follow the suggested procedures on page T5.

Group Problem Posing/Problem Solving

- Follow the suggested procedures on page T141.

Cross-Cultural Exchange

OBJECTIVE: To compare job benefits in different cultures.

- Follow the suggested procedures on page T74.
- Ask students what job benefits people receive in their other countries. Are the benefits different? How? (bonuses, etc.) Which benefits are better? Ask who pays for each of the benefits—the employer? the employee? both? Have students draw conclusions from the discussion. List their conclusions on the board.

EXPANSION

- Have small groups of students choose one of the illustrations on page 146, and write a story about it together. Then have each group read or tell the story to the class.

REVIEW

IN THE TEXT

Partner Interview

- Follow the suggested procedures on page T4.

Write

OBJECTIVE: To write about work activities in a journal entry.

- Read the instructions with the class.
- Circulate while students write their journal entries; help as needed.

Tell Your Partner

OBJECTIVE: To reinforce unit interview questions and answers.

- Students may either read their journal entry or tell their partners the information from it; whichever format they are more comfortable with.
- *Variation:* Students may read their journal to a group of five or six students or to the whole class. Encourage other students to ask questions.

EXPANSION

- Review all the transparencies or picture dictionary pages in this unit as individual **VOCABULARY CHALLENGES**. Give the class five minutes to write down all the vocabulary they can remember from a picture. (No looking in the book or at notes!) Then have them report back informally, and make a master list on the board. Have them copy from the board any words that they didn't remember into the **Vocabulary** section of their notebooks.

- •• Play a chain game. Use any word or phrase from the unit. For example, *benefits*. The next student in the chain has to think of a word beginning with *s*, such as supervisor. The next student thinks of a word beginning with *r*. Continue around the room.

UNIT TEST

- A **conversation test** and a **vocabulary test** for this unit are located in the back of this Teacher's Guide, plus suggestions for administration. Feel free to make as many copies as you need.

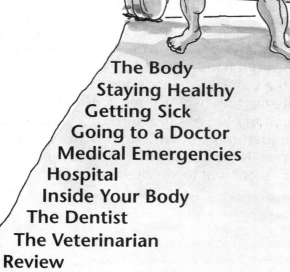

LEARNING STRATEGIES

➤ Describe a recent illness you had. How did you feel? What did you do to get well?

➤ In the Journal section of your notebook, write about your family's health. Include any medical problems, accidents, or emergencies.

THE BODY

WARM UP

- Write PARTS OF THE BODY on the board.
- Point to different parts of your body and ask *What's this?* List students' answers on the board.

IN THE TEXT

- Look at the illustrations on both pages of the text, or have the students look at the transparency with books closed.
- To introduce the vocabulary, see the suggested procedures in **TO THE TEACHER**.
- Point to the detailed parts of the body on page 151 and ask students if they know the names of these body parts.
- Not all parts of the body are included in the vocabulary list; ask students if they know any more words (*knuckle, toenail, palm*, etc.). Add these words to the list on the board or on the transparency, and have students copy them into the **Vocabulary** section of their notebooks.
- Ask whether children are allowed to write with their left hand in the students' native countries. (In the United States, in the past, all students were forced to write with their right hand.)
- Write these column headings on the board: ACTIVITY, LEFT HAND, RIGHT HAND, EITHER HAND, BOTH HANDS. Under ACTIVITY, write *write your name.* Ask students how many write with their left hand? right hand? either hand? both hands? (Students raise their hands.) Count the number of hands and write the number under the appropriate heading. Write another two or three activities on the board (*catch a ball, shake hands, eat with a fork, tie your shoes,* etc.), and poll students about them. Then ask students to suggest more activities. Continue the poll as long as students can continue thinking up activities done with the hands. Have students copy the actions into the **Vocabulary** section of their notebooks.

Group Game: *"What is it?"*

OBJECTIVE: To integrate vocabulary and ask yes/no questions about the body through an information-gap activity.

- This game is like "20 Questions," but with no set limit to the number of questions students may ask.
- Read the instructions aloud with the students.
- Demonstrate possible yes/no questions: *Is it part of the face? Is it small? Is it part of a hand? Is it part of a leg?* Write these questions on the board.
- Have students suggest other yes/no questions, and add them to the list on the board.
- Be the leader first. Say *I'm thinking of a part of the body.* Students have to ask you yes/no questions.
- When a student guesses the correct word, have that student become the new leader and the game continues.
- Divide the class into groups of six and have students play the game. Continue the game as long as interest and involvement are high.

Class Game: *"Follow the Leader"*

OBJECTIVE: To reinforce vocabulary with a total physical response (TPR) activity.

- Read each instruction aloud and demonstrate the instruction.
- Tell students to close their books, listen, and follow instructions.
- Read the instructions again, modeling the action and encouraging the students to imitate you.
- Read the instructions again; this time *do not* demonstrate the actions yourself. Have students follow the instructions. Mix up the instructions to make them more difficult.
- For further practice, have a student give the instructions and have the rest of the class follow.

EXPANSION

- Play "Simon Says." Have all students stand. Explain that students must follow commands *only* when you first say "Simon says." Demonstrate by giving a command (*Simon says touch your face*) and by following the command as you say it. Then repeat the command without the "Simon says," and without following it. Tell students they will be "out" and have to sit down if they follow the commands without "Simon says." Be the leader first. Have the last remaining student (the winner) be the next leader.

STAYING HEALTHY

WARM UP

- Ask students what they do to stay healthy. Have as many students answer as possible, and list their answers on the board. Or have one student do the writing on the board and the class help with spelling the vocabulary.

IN THE TEXT

- Look at the illustrations with the students, or show the transparency with books open.
- To introduce the vocabulary, see the suggested procedures in **TO THE TEACHER**.
- Point to each illustration and ask *Which words go with this illustration?* Have students find the word or words in the vocabulary box for each illustration.

Class Discussion

OBJECTIVE: To integrate new vocabulary into the context of the situations pictured; to listen as other students tell about their community.

- Look at each illustration with the class. Ask how many people there are, who each person is, and what they are doing.
- Have the students describe each person in detail. Ask *How old is he or she? What color is his or her hair? Is he or she healthy or unhealthy? How do you know?* etc.
- Ask students about any of these clinics in your community. If any students (or you) have been to clinics, tell the class about the experiences.

Community Activity

OBJECTIVE: To find out about clinics in your area.

- Bring in telephone directories, or copy the appropriate page out of a local directory. Have students find the number of the Board of Health.
- List together on the board all the questions you have about clinics (*Where is it? What are the hours? What does it cost?* etc.). Have students copy the questions into the **Community** section of their notebooks.
- Either make a telephone call together with the class, or assign students with partners to call the Board of Health with specific questions. (First practice asking and answering the questions as a whole class and with a partner.)
- If this was a homework assignment, have partners report on their telephone calls. Discuss the results with the class.

Group Activity

OBJECTIVE: To include everyone in the decision-making process, using health vocabulary.

- Read the instructions aloud. Have the students open their books and, in the spaces provided, write their name and an example of a healthy meal, the best kind of exercise, and the number of hours of sleep that each needs each night.
- Divide the class into groups of five. Tell students that *everyone* in the group must share their examples, and then the group must decide together which examples are the best.
- When groups have all decided, list the three different categories on the board, and ask groups what they decided.
- Have a student list five decisions from each category on the board.
- Did any of the groups have the same choices? What was the most popular healthy meal? kind of exercise? number of hours of sleep needed? Why?

EXPANSION

- Write two column headings on the board: HEALTHY LIFE and UNHEALTHY LIFE. Ask students what things they *don't* do to stay healthy. If they have difficulty thinking of suggestions, refer them to the results of the **Group Activity** for things they *do* to stay healthy, or make a few suggestions: ***Don't stay up all night. Don't smoke. Don't get drunk. Don't eat lots of sweets.*** As students give suggestions, write them on the board, and ask if anyone in the class does any of these unhealthy things.

GETTING SICK

WARM UP

- Ask the students how they are feeling today. Is anyone sick? If so, with what?
- Ask the students *Do you ever get sick? With what?* If students are not sure, suggest one or two possibilities: *a cold? a headache?* Write all their sicknesses on the board.
- Ask the students when and how often they get sick, and what they do when they get sick. Ask if anyone in the class *never* gets sick.
- Congratulate the healthy person.

IN THE TEXT

- Look at the illustrations with the students, or show the transparency with books closed.
- Ask the students if the people in these illustrations are healthy. If not, what are their problems? How can the students tell?
- To introduce the vocabulary, see the suggested procedures in **TO THE TEACHER**.
- Explain (or pantomime) the words *sneeze, dizzy, laryngitis, nauseous, allergies*.

Class Discussion

OBJECTIVE: To integrate new vocabulary into the context of students' experiences; to listen and take notes of other students' experiences.

- Take notes on this class discussion. Encourage students to take notes, too. Write three headings on the board: HEALTH PROBLEM, TREATMENT, DOCTOR? Ask the first question to review the vocabulary, then the other two questions. As you ask the class questions and students answer, fill in columns with their answers under each heading; under the DOCTOR? heading, write yes or no. Have students copy important information into the **Community** section of their notebooks.
- When the discussion is finished, orally recap the notes on the board for the students, and ask students to summarize the discussion based on the notes.

Cross-Cultural Exchange

OBJECTIVE: To compare the treatment of common ailments in different cultures.

- In this case, even if many cultures are represented in your class, there will probably be a number of different answers within a single culture. If all students are from the same country, again there will be differences, depending on local traditions and family practices. Encourage students to ask each other questions.

Group Game: *"What's the matter?"*

OBJECTIVE: To reinforce vocabulary through pantomime.

- Read the instructions together. Then divide the class into groups of four or five students. Have each group choose one student to pantomime one of the illnesses/injuries illustrated on page 154. Whoever guesses first in each group will go next.
- *Variations:* Have everyone take a turn, going around the circle. Or prepare in advance enough slips of paper, with a health problem listed on each, for the whole class. Have each student pick a slip of paper. Then divide into groups, and have everyone take a turn pantomiming. Or do this as a whole class activity, and have each student take a turn coming to the front of the class, picking a paper, and pantomiming the health problem written on it.

Partner Activity

OBJECTIVE: To practice oral and written vocabulary for common health remedies.

- Read the instructions together. Point out which bottles are empty and be sure students understand that they must fill in the labels with the names of medicines they use themselves. Tell them to draw in more bottles or boxes if they wish.
- Divide the class into pairs. For this activity it is an advantage to pair students who rarely work together or who are from different cultural backgrounds.
- Circulate; help as needed.
- When nearly everyone is finished, have each pair join another pair and share their label names. Ask the class if any pairs have written the same medicine names on any of the labels.
- Have each pair report the name of the extra medicine from their own medicine cabinet. On the board write a list of all the kinds of medicine, and have students copy the new words into the **Vocabulary** section of their notebooks.

EXPANSION

- Bring to class an assortment of over-the-counter health remedies. Hold each up and ask the class what it is and what it is used for. Then divide the class into groups and give each group one of the bottles or boxes. Write four headings on the board: MEDICINE, WHAT IS THIS MEDICINE FOR?, WHAT IS THE DOSAGE?, WHAT ARE THE WARNINGS? Explain the three questions, and give a sample answer to each from the label of one of the medicines. Ask each group to find the answers to the three questions and report to the class. Circulate; help as needed. When everyone is finished, have each group report their answers, and have one person from each group write the answers on the board.

GOING TO A DOCTOR

WARM UP

- Ask students where or how they find doctors. Do they ask friends or relatives for referrals? Do they ever use a telephone directory to find a doctor?
- Ask students what kinds of doctors they can find in the directories. Have them spell each specialty for you as you write it on the board. When you have finished, have students copy the list into the **Vocabulary** section of their notebooks.

IN THE TEXT

- With the students, look at the page from the telephone list in the text.
- Help the students with the pronunciation of the medical terms.
- Ask students what the abbreviations mean.
- Provide additional terms, such as names of specialists. (*A doctor of pediatrics is a pediatrician.*)

Group Decision

OBJECTIVE: To practice vocabulary in a decision-making context.

- Read the instructions aloud. Have the students list the possible physicians to visit for each of the health problems.
- Divide the class into groups of five or six.
- Have *everyone* in the group share their list and suggest a doctor for each of the six medical problems.
- Then have the groups decide together which doctor to visit. Have them consider things like accessibility and familiarity in making their decision. (*Do you know the doctor? Is he or she a good doctor? How far away is the doctor?* etc.) Have each group write the appropriate doctor in the space provided.
- When all groups have decided, list the different medical problems on the board. Ask groups what they decided. Have a student list decisions on the board. Were there any differences in the decisions? What were the differences based on?

Partner Role Play

OBJECTIVE: To write and role play a conversation to make an appointment with a doctor.

- Divide the class into pairs. Tell the class that each pair must decide on a doctor to visit and a reason for the visit.
- Read the sample questions from the page together. Check for pronunciation.
- With the class, create some sample questions for the *receptionist* or *answering service* to ask the *patient*. Write the questions on the board, and have students copy them into the **Activities** section of their notebooks.
- Ask for or suggest sample answers to each question.
- Have students decide who will be the patient and who will be the receptionist or the answering service.
- Circulate; help as needed.
- When most are finished, either have every pair read their conversation in front of the class, or divide into groups of four pairs and have each pair read their conversation to their group. Have each group select one conversation to be read to the whole class.

Write

OBJECTIVE: To reinforce written vocabulary on Patient Information Forms.

- Read the instructions and the form with your class. Make sure students understand what they need to write on each line.
- Fill in a sample form for yourself on the board or on the transparency. Have students imagine a medical problem—it's easiest to choose one that they have really had.
- Circulate; help as needed.

Partner Role Play

OBJECTIVE: To write and role play a first visit to a doctor.

- Divide the class into pairs. Read the instructions together. Have students decide who will be the *patient* and who will be the *doctor*. The student who is the patient will use his or her **Patient Information Form** for this role play.
- Follow the suggested procedures for the previous **Partner Role Play**.

EXPANSION

- Role play a return visit to the same doctor a week later. Have the partners decide whether the patient's situation will be better or worse than it was at the first visit.

MEDICAL EMERGENCIES

WARM UP

- Bring in newspaper and magazine illustrations and stories of accidents; show them to the students. Talk about what happened and list vocabulary on the board.
- Ask students what kinds of medical emergencies they know about. List all the kinds they can think of.

IN THE TEXT

- Look at the illustrations with the students, or show the transparency with books closed.
- To introduce the vocabulary, see the suggested procedures in **TO THE TEACHER**.

Class Discussion

OBJECTIVE: **To integrate new vocabulary into the context of strip stories, discuss what to do in medical emergencies, and listen to other students' experiences.**

- Ask students what is happening in each of these illustrations. Write picture captions on the board if you wish. Or keep this activity entirely oral and let the students do the writing in groups later as a review activity (see **EXPANSION**). In either case, have students use the new vocabulary to tell the stories.
- Ask the students what they would do in these situations. Would they do the same? something different? Discuss the possibilities.
- Ask if anyone in the class has ever had a medical emergency. Have everyone who says yes tell the class briefly about the emergency.

Partner Activity

OBJECTIVE: To decide with a partner how to solve medical emergency problems.

- Make sure all students understand each situation. Use situation 1 as an example, and help them decide as a class what to do.
- Divide the class into pairs. Each pair should decide what to do in each situation.
- When they are finished, have pairs report all the different solutions they have chosen. Write them all on the board. Decide as a class which ones are best.

Group Decision

OBJECTIVE: To use first aid vocabulary to make decisions with a group about medical emergency treatment.

- Bring in an "official" first aid kit and take out the contents. Write individual index cards with the vocabulary for all the contents. Put the kit supplies on a table. Hand out the cards to students, and have them come up to the table and match their card with one of the first aid supplies.
- Divide the class into groups of five and have them decide which supplies are needed for each emergency.
- When they are finished, have each group report their decisions.
- Write the decisions on the board. Compare different solutions to the emergencies. Which choices does the class think are best?

Community Activity

OBJECTIVE: To clarify important information about local emergency facilities.

- As you ask these questions, write students' answers on the board whenever they are generally applicable. Have students copy important information into the **Community** section of their notebooks.
- If students do not know whether their insurance covers emergency room visits (Question 4), direct them to find out by calling the insurance company or by asking someone at home who is responsible for medical bills, etc. You may prefer to have students report on this question in writing to avoid possible embarrassment.

EXPANSION

- As a review of vocabulary, divide the class into small groups to write captions for each of the four medial emergency strip stories. When they are finished, have each group read their captions to the class.

- •• Have groups role play each of the medical emergencies illustrated. Each student should play a role.

HOSPITAL

WARM UP

- Ask students the reasons people go to the hospital as patients, and whether each is an "in-patient" or an "out-patient" service.
- Ask students if they have ever stayed overnight in a hospital. Ask how many days they stayed. If students seem willing to discuss their hospital experience, have them tell the story, but be careful with these questions since they may be too personal for some students.
- *Variation:* Ask students if they have ever visited anyone in the hospital, and have them tell the class about the situation.

IN THE TEXT

- Look at the illustration with the students, or show the transparency.
- To introduce the vocabulary, see the suggested procedures in **TO THE TEACHER**.
- Explain *coma, unconscious*.

What's the Story?

- Follow the suggested procedures on page T23.

Class Discussion

- Follow the suggested procedures on page T29.

Partner Activity

OBJECTIVE: To understand hospital signs.

- Look at the hospital sign illustrations with the class. Ask students what each sign means. *If you follow the sign, what will you find? What do people do in that place?* Elicit as many possibilities from students as you can.
- With the class, read the five situations and make sure that all students understand all the vocabulary for each situation. Then divide the class into pairs.
- Have each pair decide which sign to follow for each situation. When they have finished, have them report their decisions to the class.

EXPANSION

- Have pairs create role plays to ask for and give directions for each of the situations in the Partner Activity above. Write a model conversation on the board first:

  (A) *Excuse me, I'm looking for the gift shop. Could you tell me how to get there?*
  (B) *Sure. Go to the end of this corridor and turn right.*
  (A) *Go to the end of this corridor and turn right?*
  (B) *That's it.*
  (A) *Thank you.*
  (B) *No problem.*

- •• Ask students if anyone has been in hospitals in more than one country. If they have, ask them what differences they noticed. List the differences on the board. If they are willing, have them tell the stories of their hospital experiences to the class.

- Review the first aid kit supplies vocabulary with the whole class, write it on the board, and have students copy it into the **Community** section of their notebooks.

INSIDE YOUR BODY

WARM UP

- Ask the students *What is inside our bodies? inside the head? inside the arms? inside the chest?* Students may already know some of the vocabulary. Encourage them to guess at words they are not sure of; they may come close. List on the board all the organs and other body parts they can think of.
- *Variation:* Draw a picture of the body with some common shapes (heart, kidneys, lungs). Have students guess the names of the shapes.

IN THE TEXT

- Look at the illustration with the students, or show the transparency with books closed.
- To introduce the vocabulary, see the suggested procedures in **TO THE TEACHER**.
- Make sure students understand which body part each vocabulary word really represents. The easiest way to make inner body part vocabulary clear is to discuss common medical problems associated with each body part. Write the heading MEDICAL PROBLEMS on the board, and have the students elicit medical problems associated with certain body parts. Write the new words and have students copy them into the **Vocabulary** section of their notebooks.
- Discuss the function of the body part to help clarify it. Expand or limit this discussion to fit your students' and your own familiarity with human anatomy and physiology.
- Ask students if anyone they know—their family, friends, or neighbors—has ever had a problem with any of these parts of the body. Have them tell the story. If there is new vocabulary, add it to the list on the board.
- Leave this list on the board. It is to be used for the **Group Activity**, page 163.

Group Activity

OBJECTIVE: To associate vocabulary for medical problems with the corresponding body part, and follow written instructions.

- Divide the class into groups of five or six students. Read the instructions with the class and make sure they understand them. Point out that each of them must come up with the name of a body part associated with the medical problem. Refer the students to the list of Medical Problems on the board.
- Have a *reporter* from each group read their answers to the class.
- Ask if anyone can think of any other medical problems that "go with" parts of the body. Create a chart on the board like the one in the book.

Cross-Cultural Exchange

OBJECTIVE: To compare medical treatment in different cultures.

- If many cultures are represented in your class, one or two students can answer for each cultural group. However, as with all medical issues, students are likely to disagree about practices, so you may have a lively discussion. If all students are from the same country, disagreement is still probable. Encourage them to understand the differences.
- Have students decide as a class which treatments sound best after they discuss each medical problem. At the end of the activity, draw conclusions from the discussion.

Group Game: *"Gossip!"*

OBJECTIVE: To listen to and repeat a story with details, using new vocabulary.

- Follow the suggested procedures on page T63.

   Last week a nineteen-year-old girl came to the hospital with her aunt. The girl was very weak and very tired. Her blood tests showed a problem, but she did not want treatment. Her religion was against medical treatment. The girl's aunt was angry. She said, "You must have treatment!" The girl said, "No. God will give me treatment." Then she and her aunt went away. They did not come back, so we don't know what happened.

EXPANSION

- Make up a **Find Someone Who** activity, or have the class make one up. Include things like: has had a broken bone, likes hospitals, takes vitamins every day, etc. Follow the suggested procedures on page T12.

THE DENTIST

WARM UP

- Bring toothpaste, a toothbrush, and dental floss to class.
- Ask the students what the items are and how to use them. Ask what to do first, what second, what third. As they tell you, pantomime the process. When you have finished, have students repeat the steps; write the steps on the board.
- Ask students why they go to the dentist. List on the board all the reasons they give.

IN THE TEXT

- Look at the illustration with the students, or show the transparency with books open.
- To introduce the vocabulary, see the suggested procedures in **TO THE TEACHER.**
- Discuss the words *cavity, extraction, abscess.*

Partner Interview

- Follow the suggested procedures on page T4.

Cross-Cultural Exchange

OBJECTIVE: To compare dental treatment in different cultures.

- Follow the suggested procedures on page T74.

Partner Role Play

OBJECTIVE: To write and perform a role play in which to review new vocabulary and structures in a given context.

- Follow the suggested procedures on page T93.

What's the Story?

OBJECTIVE: To create a group story using dentist-visit situations and vocabulary.

- Divide the class into groups of five students. Read the instructions aloud and discuss the illustration on page 164 together. Make sure the students understand that they must tell about only *one* patient in the illustration in their story. Since there are ten questions to answer on page 165, have groups assign two questions to each student.
- Follow the suggested procedures on page T23.

Cross-Cultural Exchange

OBJECTIVE: To compare dentistry and baby teeth customs across cultures.

- Ask students if they know the custom of the Tooth Fairy. If not, have them look at the illustrations on page 165 and describe them to you.
- Have a number of students explain their family practices about baby teeth.
- Have students draw conclusions from the discussion. Are the baby teeth practices dependent on family traditions or on ethnic groups?

EXPANSION

- Ask about the students' dental visits. *How often do you go to the dentist? Did you go as a child? How much do you like to go?* etc.

THE VETERINARIAN

WARM UP

- Before this class, ask if any students have pets. If the answer is yes, ask them to bring something to class that is relevant (the pet's leash, toy, or photo). If you have a pet, bring in as much realia as you can, such as pet food, pet's toys, etc.
- Ask students *What do veterinarians do? Why do people go to them? Have you ever gone to a veterinarian? What for?*
- *Variation:* Have students do a **Vocabulary Challenge**. Give them five minutes to write lists of as many animals as they can think of. When they are finished, have them read the lists. Make a master list of ANIMALS on the board and have students copy it into the **Vocabulary** section of their notebooks.

IN THE TEXT

- Look at the illustration with the students, or show the transparency with books closed.
- Ask students where this scene takes place and what things they see. Make a list on the board of all the vocabulary generated.
- To introduce the vocabulary, see the suggested procedures in **TO THE TEACHER**.

Class Discussion

OBJECTIVE: To integrate new vocabulary into the context of students' experiences; to listen to other students' experiences and take notes.

- Follow the suggested procedures on page T29.

What's the Story?

- Follow the suggested procedures on page T23.

Group Problem Posing/Problem Solving

OBJECTIVE: To clarify a problem and figure out a solution.

- Read the instructions aloud. Look at the illustrations together and ask students what things they see. Put any new vocabulary on the board, but do not state the problems.
- Divide the class into groups of three or four. Tell students that each group must figure out and explain exactly what problem one of the illustrations shows, and then decide on the best solution together. Explain that they must include details in their solution.
- Circulate; help as needed. When they have finished, have each group select a *reporter* to tell/read the problem and the solution to the class. Encourage other groups to ask questions.

Speech

- Follow the suggested procedures on page T33.

EXPANSION

- Ask students what they feed their pets. Use the ANIMALS list on the board, or recreate it if need be, and make a corresponding list of FOODS. Include the animals' favorite foods as well as what they are regularly fed.

REVIEW

IN THE TEXT

Crossword Puzzle

OBJECTIVE: To review vocabulary for basic parts of the body.

- Divide the class into pairs. Explain ACROSS and DOWN, and that students need to write words in the boxes to match the illustrations below.
- Circulate; help as needed.
- When they are finished, have students spell the correct answers aloud as a class, and write the answers on the board.

EXPANSION

- Review all the transparencies or picture dictionary pages in this unit as individual **VOCABULARY CHALLENGES**. Give the class five minutes to write down all the vocabulary they can remember from an illustration. (No looking in the book or at notes!) Then have them report back informally, and make a master list on the board. Have them copy from the board any words that they didn't remember.

UNIT TEST

- A **conversation test** and a **vocabulary test** for this unit are located in the back of this Teacher's Guide, plus suggestions for administration. Feel free to make as many copies as you need.

UNIT 10

LEISURE

LEARNING STRATEGIES

➤ In the Journal section of your notebook, write about your daily leisure activities. For example: I took a walk; I played soccer; I read; I went to a movie.

➤ Find a new leisure activity to practice your English. For example: Watch TV shows in English with a friend. Discuss the shows in English; Take a walk with a friend. Pick a topic and discuss in English.

LEISURE TIME

WARM UP

- Bring in as much realia as you can: movie schedule, *TV Guide*, library book, cassette, guitar, balls, etc. Ask the students to bring in something that represents their leisure activities.
- Write two column headings on the board: THINGS WE USE and LEISURE ACTIVITIES.
- Ask students to name items for the category. List the vocabulary on the board under THINGS WE USE. Ask students what leisure activities the items are used for. List this vocabulary under LEISURE ACTIVITIES. Have students copy the new words into the **Vocabulary** section of their notebooks.

IN THE TEXT

- Look at the illustrations on both pages of the text, or show the transparency with student books closed.
- To introduce vocabulary, see the suggested procedures in **TO THE TEACHER**.
- Ask students if any of the leisure activities or things people are using in the illustrations match words listed on the board. Review the words that match. Then ask what the other people are doing, and what they are using. Add any new vocabulary to the lists on the board.
- Ask students if they like any of these leisure activities *Do you like to swim?* etc. You may either skim over these preference questions quickly or poll class preferences and write numbers on the board.

Group Vocabulary Challenge

- Follow the suggested procedure on page T17, but divide the class into groups of five or six rather than four.

Group Survey

- Follow the suggested procedures on page T19.

Partner Interview

- Follow the suggested procedures on page T4.

What's the Story?

OBJECTIVE: To create a group story using the leisure time situation.

- Follow the suggested procedures on page T23.

EXPANSION

- Discuss what leisure activities are popular with the students. Make a list of these activities on the board. If several countries are represented in the class, have students from each country tell the class about popular activities in their country or hometown.

•• Go back to the realia from the beginning of this lesson. Hold up each item and ask the class *What is this? What do we do with it?* Have students volunteer to demonstrate the use of each item.

••• As homework, direct students to write an entry in the **Journal** section of their notebooks about one or more of their favorite leisure activities. Help one student create a model entry on the board. In the next class session, have students read their entries to a partner or to a small group. Or collect the entries, read them to the class yourself, and have students guess who wrote each entry.

GOING OUT

WARM UP

- Write SATURDAY NIGHT on the board. Ask students if this is special to them. Do they go out? Ask students where they go and what they do. Make lists of places/events and actions.
- Bring in the entertainment section of a local newspaper. Discuss the activities listed. Were any of them ones the students had suggested?

IN THE TEXT

- Look at the illustrations on both pages of the text, or show the transparency with student books closed.
- To introduce the vocabulary, see the suggested procedures in **TO THE TEACHER**.

Class Discussion

OBJECTIVE: To integrate new vocabulary into a discussion of captioning.

- This activity may be done as a whole-class discussion. Or begin it with a group discussion by dividing the class into groups of five or six. Direct each group to write possible captions for each spot drawing.
- Write a number for each illustration on the board. Either have groups report suggested captions, or ask for suggestions from anyone in the class. As students answer, write their captions under the correct number.
- As a class, discuss how to choose the best captions. What questions should the captions answer? (who, what, where, when, why) Decide together what the class thinks is most appropriate.

Find Someone Who

- Follow the suggested procedures on page T12.

Partner Role Play

OBJECTIVE: To invite, accept or refuse, and negotiate an invitation to go out and do something.

- Ask students to name events or activities that they might invite someone to. Have a *recorder* write the possibilities on the board for students to copy into the **Activities** section of their notebooks.
- Model a possible phone invitation to an event listed on the board. Include phrases such as *Would you like to. . . ? That sounds like fun. When it is? Where is it? What time does it start?*
- Follow the suggested procedures on page T93.

Community Activity

OBJECTIVE: To become familiar with the details of local events.

- Have students bring in newspapers (or use the newspapers from the **Warm Up**) and flyers telling about local events that will happen soon.
- Divide the class into informal groups to look at the entertainment sections of the papers.
- While students are finding events, write headlines on the board: EVENT, PLACE, DATE, TIME, COST, HOW TO GET THERE.
- Have groups report all events they find, and copy details on the board. Have the class copy the information into the **Community** section of their notebooks.

EXPANSION

- Ask students what events they have recently attended. Have a student who attended an interesting event sit at the front of the class. Have the class take turns asking questions about the event: What was it? Where was it? When was it? etc.

WATCHING TELEVISION

WARM UP

- Bring in *TV Guides* or guides from newspapers or magazines. (You will need enough of them for each group in the **Community Activity** on page 175.)
- Write column headings on the board: TV PROGRAM, DAY, TIME, and CHANNEL. Leave space for a fifth column.
- Ask students what they watch on TV. List the programs, days, times, and channels under the appropriate headings.

IN THE TEXT

- Look at the illustration with the students, or show the transparency with student books closed.
- To introduce the vocabulary, see the suggested procedures in **TO THE TEACHER**.
- Write TYPE as a fifth column heading in the remaining space on the board. Ask students *Which is a commercial? a mystery? a soap opera? a game show? a variety show? a talk show? a sports program? a comedy? sad? funny? news?* Fill in the TYPE column. Add more categories if needed.

What's the Story?

- Make sure that everyone understands that they must include in their group's story all the characters in the picture—the people, the dogs, as well as the television program the woman is watching.
- Follow the suggested procedures on page T23.

Group Decision

OBJECTIVE: To discuss and decide as a group what the people in the picture prefer.

- Read the instructions aloud. Have students list, in the **Activities** section of their notebooks, the kind of video they think each person in the picture would prefer.
- Have students stay in their same groups of five from the previous exercise. Tell students that *everyone* in the group must share their lists and *together* decide what kind of video each person in the illustration would prefer to watch alone and what kind they would enjoy watching together.
- When all groups have decided, ask each to choose a *reporter* and report their decisions to the class. Do all the groups agree? If not, discuss the differences as a class.

Partner Interview

OBJECTIVE: To ask, answer, take notes, and listen to answers about TV and videos.

- Follow the suggested procedures on page T4.

Community Activity

OBJECTIVE: To use a real TV schedule.

- This activity can be done with a partner, in small groups, or as a whole-class activity. Provide as many copies of the TV schedule as possible, and set up groups accordingly.
- When students report their choices to the class, practice pronouncing names of TV shows together.
- If you wish, you may end the activity with an informal class poll to see what the class as a whole would choose to watch.

EXPANSION

- If a television is available in your classroom, check a newspaper TV schedule to see what programs are on during your class. Explain what the choices are, and by consensus choose a channel to watch together. If you are able to videotape the program as you watch it, watch a five- or ten-minute segment without pausing, then ask students what they have understood. Replay the tape in short segments (not more than 30 seconds each).

MOVIES

WARM UP

- Ask students what their favorite movies are. Write the movie titles on the board. Ask how many others in the class have ever seen that movie, and whether they liked it.
- (You may have discussed favorite movies already, during your discussion of videos. If so, this can be a review/warm up combined, or you may want to focus on a different question, such as how often students go to the movies, or whether they prefer to watch videos at home or go out to a movie theater, and why.)

IN THE TEXT

- Look at the illustration with the students, or show the transparency with student books closed.
- Tell the students they're all going to the movies. Ask them what they should do first. What next? Then what? As you ask, write these questions on the board: **What movie do you want to see? Where is the movie playing? How much does a ticket cost? How many tickets do we need?** (Have everyone count the number of students in the class, then point to the ticket window and say (*number*), **please.**) **Do you want something to eat? What?** (Point to the refreshment stand and ask students for the vocabulary: *popcorn*, etc.) **What do you want to do while we're waiting for the movie to begin?** (Point to the video games, rest rooms, and discuss.) **Where do you want to sit?** (Point to the seats.) **Do you like this actor and actress?** (Point to the screen.) **Are you comfortable? Can you see the screen?**

Class Discussion

OBJECTIVE: To discuss experiences with movies and take notes.

- Tell the students to take notes in the **Activities** section of their notebooks. Write five headings on the board: LAST MOVIE, NEW MOVIES, WANT TO SEE, EAT/DRINK, VIDEO GAMES. As you ask the class questions and students answer, fill in columns under each heading, and discuss different answers. When the discussion is finished, recap the notes orally.

Group Role Play

OBJECTIVE: To write a group dialog about a movie-going situation, and combine verbal and non-verbal simulation practice.

- Discuss four possible situations with the class. (What things might the two friends say to each other? What do people say to a ticket seller? What conversations might take place at the refreshment stand? What could happen with an usher collecting tickets?)
- Follow the suggested procedures on page T69.
- *Variation:* If you prefer, this role play can be done as a puppet show. Make hand puppets with small paper bags, and use a table and sheet for a stage.

Conversation Squares

- Follow the suggested procedures on page T33.

EXPANSION

- Are movie theaters the same in the students' countries? (Are there video games in the lobby? What things do people eat and drink at the movies? etc.) What movies are most popular there? What actors? What comedians?

- • Bring in a newspaper and check its movie guide. Choose a movie to see as a class, arrange time and transportation, and go to the movie together.

INDIVIDUAL SPORTS

WARM UP

- Ask students what words for individual sports they know. On the board, list all the words they can think of, or have a student list words as the class suggests them. Have everyone help with the spelling.

IN THE TEXT

- Look at the illustrations with the students, or show the transparency with student books closed.
- Ask students about each individual sport:

  How many have ever tried this sport?
  If you haven't tried this sport, would you like to?
  Why/Why not?
  Do you ever watch any of these sports?
  Do you watch them on TV?
  Have you ever watched the Olympics?
  What sport do you enjoy watching most?

- Note that these questions may lead to an extended class discussion of student likes and dislikes. Encourage the discussion, as it will lead into the next activity, a **Group Survey**.

Group Survey

- Follow the suggested procedures on page T19.
- Point out that the questions in this survey are open-ended. There may be a variety of answers.
- Set a time limit for each question.

Class Game: *"What is your favorite way to exercise?"*

- Follow the suggested procedures on page T17.

Community Activity

OBJECTIVE: To find out about local sports facilities.

- This can be used as an in-class activity or as an out-of-class assignment. If it is out-of-class, students can use their home telephone directories. If it is in-class, you will need to provide enough telephone directories (or copies of relevant pages) for groups to work with, or make transparencies of relevant pages for the entire class.
- Show the class the YELLOW PAGES section of the telephone directory. Look up the first facility, *skating rink*, together, and discuss the category in the directory under which you found *skating rink*. Write down the address and telephone number, if there is one, of the skating rink. If there isn't one, look for the next facility together.
- Have students—either in groups, as a class, or at home—complete the activity and share their answers.
- Have students copy relevant information into the **Community** section of their notebooks.

EXPANSION

- Decide as a class on a physical activity that everyone would like to do or watch together (or some do and others watch). Make a list on the board of information you will need (days and hours open? cost? special group rates? available transportation? food and other facilities? etc.). Go on the outing together and enjoy!

- •• Have students write a journal entry about an individual athlete they admire. Who is the athlete? What does he or she play? Why is he or she special? Have students read their journal entries to a group, or collect the journals, read them to the class, and have students guess who wrote each one.

TEAM SPORTS

WARM UP

- Bring to class a few copies of the sports section of a major newspaper. Distribute them to groups of students informally. Ask students what team sports they see in the papers. List on the board all the team sports that students can name.
- Ask students about other team sports not in the newspaper. Add these to the list.
- Start at the top of the list. Ask *How many students like this team sport? Do you like to play it? Do you like to watch it? Do you watch professional teams? local teams? high school teams? children's teams? Do you go to games? Do you watch games on TV? When are the games?*
- (This **WARM UP** previews student interest and experience with team sports. Draw as much vocabulary and information from the class as you can during the **WARM UP** so that you will know the most appropriate direction for your class to go with the rest of the topic.)

IN THE TEXT

- Look at the illustrations with the students, or show the transparency with student books closed.
- Some of this vocabulary may be difficult for students to understand if they are unfamiliar with the particular team sport. You may want to draw diagrams on the board or use illustrations from your picture file to clarify concepts and show how the game is played. You may ask students who are familiar with the game to come to the front of the class and demonstrate (pantomime) words like *pitch, dribble, pass, tackle*, etc. Or, if you have a student who plays one of these team sports, you may have the student teach the vocabulary for the sport.
- Are any students interested in any other team sports in your list on the board? If so, ask students for basic vocabulary for each of these additional sports, and list the vocabulary on the board next to each team sport. Ask questions like *What equipment do they use? What do they do with it? What is a goal called in this sport? How do the players get a goal?*

Group Discussion

- Follow the suggested procedures on page T49. Alternatively, this activity can be structured as a **Partner Interview** (suggested procedures on page T4).

Conversation Squares

OBJECTIVE: To interview classmates about their favorite team sports.

- Follow the suggested procedures on page T33.

Community Activity

OBJECTIVE: To become aware of team sports seasons, watch a game on TV, and report on it.

- Ask students if they know what sport season it is, and which teams are involved.
- Bring in a *TV Guide* or ask students if there is an important game coming up on TV. Find out the date, time, and channel of the game.
- Assign the students to watch at least part of the game on TV and to write a summary of the game.
- In the class following the game, have students report orally on what happened.

Cross-Cultural Exchange

OBJECTIVE: To compare team sports and sports heroes in different countries.

- Follow the suggested procedures on page T74.

EXPANSION

- Depending on facilities available to you, have your class decide on a team sport to play together, such as volleyball or softball. Form teams, review the rules, and play a game.

AT THE PARK

WARM UP

- With books closed, ask the students if they ever go to a park, what parks they go to, where the parks are, what they see there, and what they do there. As the students answer, write new vocabulary on the board.

IN THE TEXT

- Look at the illustrations on both pages of the text, or show the transparencies with student books closed.
- To introduce the vocabulary, see the suggested procedures in **TO THE TEACHER**.
- Ask students *What do you see in this park? Does this park look like the parks you know? What is the same? What is different?*
- Write headings SIMILARITIES and DIFFERENCES on the board. List student responses under each heading. These questions may lead to discussion of differences in flowers, trees, animals, birds, benches, park sizes, park activities, park lighting, etc., with many additional new words. If students have difficulty explaining these differences, have them draw the different flower, animal, etc., on the board for clarification.

Find Someone Who

- Follow the suggested procedures on page T12.

Strip Story

OBJECTIVE: To make decisions about a strip story with a group and to write captions together.

- Divide the class into groups of four. Tell students they must decide answers to these questions: *What are the names of the people in these pictures? Where is the park? What month is it? what day of the week? What are the people doing?*
- Next, have each group decide on captions for the illustrations that include their answers to the questions above.
- Finally, have each group choose a *reporter* to read their captions to the class.
- With the class decide on the best captions.

Cross-Cultural Exchange

OBJECTIVE: To share information about parks in different countries.

- Follow the suggested procedures on page T74.

EXPANSION

- Plan to go to a park together. This can be a field trip to a famous park in your area, or a short walk to a local park. Plan together what you will do in the park: play Frisbee? have a picnic? take photographs of each other? do a partner interview? observe people in the park and take notes? etc.

- ●● Have partners write a conversation that takes place in the park and present it to the class or to a group as a puppet show or role play. The conversation may be between the two students, or they may make up two other people or even two animals—this is an opportunity for students to use their imagination!

TAKING A TRIP

WARM UP

- Collect brochures from travel agents, bring them to class, and lay them out on a table before class.
- As students come in, have them choose a brochure that looks interesting, take it to their seat, and study it. When everyone has had time to review the brochures, ask each student to tell the class about the trip it describes.
- *Variation:* Divide the class into groups. Have each group pick a brochure, study it, and tell the class about this trip. Each student in the group must say one sentence.
- Write TIMES AROUND THE WORLD on the board. Ask the class *What time is it now? What time is it in your country? What time is it in California? New York? Denver? Chicago? Miami? (Vancouver? Montreal? Toronto?)* Write each city/state and the time on the board, and have students copy it in the **Community** section of their notebooks.
- Ask *Do you ever go on long trips? Where do you go? How do you get there? How long does it take?* Discuss answers.

IN THE TEXT

- Look at the illustration with the students, or show the transparency with student books closed.
- To introduce the vocabulary, see the suggested procedures in **TO THE TEACHER**.
- Map study: Have the students find the maps in the **student book APPENDIX**. Then have them look at each map and together pronounce some of the places on the maps. Ask if anyone in the class has ever been any place on that map. Have the student describe the place for the class. *What is the climate like? What does it look like?* etc.

What's the Story?

- Follow the suggested procedures on page T23.
- Write these questions on the board and read them together: *Where is this woman going? What is her name? What is she packing in her suitcase? What will the weather be like on her trip? How will she travel? What will she do there? How long will she stay? Who is going with her? Will she have a good time?*

Group Vocabulary Challenge

- Follow the suggested procedures on page T17.

Group Discussion

- Follow the suggested procedures on page T49.

Write

OBJECTIVE: To review vocabulary of travel greetings.

- Read the instructions with your class.
- Write a sample postcard on the board, with students providing suggestions to fill in the blanks. Be sure to include the address of your class!
- Circulate; help as needed.
- Have students read their greetings to the class.
- Write phrases on the board for students to copy into the **Vocabulary** section of their notebooks.

Cross-Cultural Exchange

OBJECTIVE: To compare favorite or special vacation places in different countries.

- Follow suggested procedures on page T74.
- *Variation:* Do this activity as a formal speech, using the **SPEECH** and **AUDIENCE EVALUATION** Forms.

EXPANSION

- Have students tell about trips they have taken, demonstrating with postcards, photos, and souvenirs. Bring your own memorabilia to the class and tell about a trip. Have students ask you questions about the trip.

- •• Choose a place that you haven't discussed yet (the Grand Canyon? Mt. Everest?) and have students (in groups) list all the things they would pack for a trip to that place. Have them read their lists to the class and make a master list on the board.

- ••• Play a **Gossip Game** (see page T63 for a description of how to play this game). Secret:

    Last winter I took a trip to a beautiful, tropical island. I stayed for one week. I had a wonderful time. Then I got on the airplane to go back home. The airplane was very crowded. Suddenly, the flight attendant said, "Attention, please. There are too many people on this plane. Who will get off?" Immediately, I got off the plane. I stayed one more day on the island. The airline company gave me a new ticket and four hundred dollars! What a wonderful trip!

AT THE BEACH

WARM UP

- Ask students to bring in tapes of music they would like to listen to at the beach.
- Bring beach paraphernalia: pail, shovel, sunscreen, beach towel, blanket, and a boombox. Have students help you set up a beach scene with the paraphernalia. Put some beach music on the boombox (everyone decide together what tape to play).
- Have the class close their eyes. Describe a beach scene: *Imagine we're at the beach today. It's a bright, sunny day, and the weather is hot. You have come out of the water, and you are lying on a blanket with your eyes closed. A cool breeze is blowing. You can feel the breeze and smell the salt water. The sand is warm. The sun is hot. You can hear people around you. What are they doing?*
- Have students tell you what everyone at the beach is doing. Write the vocabulary on the board. Have students open their eyes. Ask *How do you feel now?*

IN THE TEXT

- Look at the illustration with the students, or show the transparency with student books closed.
- To introduce the vocabulary, see the suggested procedures in **TO THE TEACHER**.

What's the Story?

- Follow suggested procedures on page T23.
- *Variation:* Have students work with partners, asking each other *Who are you? Where are you? What are you doing? Tell me about your day at the beach.* Then have them write the stories and read them to a group.

EXPANSION

- Are there beautiful beaches in the students' countries? Have them tell the names of the beaches and describe the beaches. *What color is the sand? Are there rocks or trees? Is the water warm or cold? Are there sharks? What body of water is the beach at? What do people do there? Are there shops? How is the beach special?*

CAMPING

WARM UP

- Ask students *Have you ever gone camping? Do you know anyone who goes camping?*
- Ask questions about where they can go camping, what they can do there, and what equipment they need.
- Show calendar pictures or slides of national parks in the United States/Canada, and discuss relevant environmental issues.

IN THE TEXT

- Look at the illustrations with the students, or show the transparency with student books closed.
- To introduce the vocabulary, see the suggested procedures in **TO THE TEACHER**.
- Tell the story or ask the class what is happening. Give names to the family.
- Write WILD ANIMALS on the board. Create a list as the stories are told.

Partner Activity

OBJECTIVE: To create a story outcome with a partner.

- Have students choose a partner. Have them write captions for each illustration, decide together on an ending to the story, write it, and read it to the class.
- *Variation:* Do the captions as a class, then have pairs create story endings.

Class Discussion

OBJECTIVE: To discuss experiences with wild animals.

- Ask the three questions, and make sure as many students as possible get to answer. List new vocabulary words on the board.
- Review the wild-animal vocabulary from the illustration. Ask students if they ever see any of these wild animals, and where they see them. Ask what kinds of birds they see. Have them describe the local birds, and if you know the names of the birds they are describing, write them on the board.
- Ask if any students have ever had any experience with a wild animal. Have them tell the class their stories.

EXPANSION

- Have students tell about national parks or other recreation areas in their countries.

THE LIBRARY

WARM UP

- Bring in (or have students bring in) a library card and library book. Show them to the class.
- Explain procedures for getting a library card and borrowing library books at the public library and/or school library. List the procedures in order on the board, and have students copy them into the **Community** section of their notebooks.
- Ask students *Do you ever go to the library? What do you do there? Whom do you go with? How long do you stay? Do any of the library workers speak your native language?*

IN THE TEXT

- Look at the illustration with the students, or show the transparency with student books closed.
- To introduce the vocabulary, see the suggested procedures in **TO THE TEACHER**.
- Point to each of the people in the library and ask the class *Who is he or she? What is he or she doing?*
- Explain *periodical, encyclopedia, due, overdue, fiction, nonfiction, biography.*

Partner Vocabulary Challenge

OBJECTIVE: To review action verbs and describe people.

- Divide the class into pairs.
- Instruct students to make one list per pair of words of the people in the library and what they are doing.
- Have each pair compare lists with another pair.
- Ask several pairs to present their lists to the class.
- Write a master list on the board.

Community Activity

OBJECTIVE: To plan a visit to the local public (or school) library.

- Call or visit the library to discuss arrangements for your visit before you present it to the class.
- Discuss the library tour arrangements with your class. List all details of the tour on the board and have students copy the list into the **Community** section of their notebooks. Arrange transportation together, if necessary.
- What information do the students need to know? For example, where is the card catalog, where are the reference books, etc.
- Visit the library, get cards, and borrow a book.

EXPANSION

- Have students bring in the book they borrowed from the library and tell the class about it.

- •• Have students volunteer to pantomime the library picture scene. Have the rest of the class give directions for the pantomime.

SCHOOL

WARM UP

- Ask students what local schools are in their neighborhoods. Write the names of the schools on the board. Ask *Who attends each of the schools? How old are the students?*

IN THE TEXT

- Look at the illustration with the students, or show the transparency with student books closed.
- Ask students what class is illustrated. Does it look interesting?
- Have the class write a story about the illustration, or divide the class into groups to write stories and read them aloud.

Group Discussion

OBJECTIVE: To discuss other courses of study.

- Write names of other courses on the board as students give answers. Have many students answer the questions.
- Ask about students' native countries. *Who goes to school? What can non-matriculated students study? Do students take courses for fun?*

Group Game: *"Gossip!"*

- Follow the suggested procedures on page T63.

> *In January, I started a computer course at a community college. The first class was very difficult. After class, my car didn't start. It was snowing and cold. I was very unhappy. Fortunately, a student from my class helped me with my car. He helped me with the computer course, too. We studied together all semester. I got an "A" in the course, and next week we are getting married! What a wonderful semester!*

Community Activity

OBJECTIVE: To discover what courses are available.

- Get catalogs, brochures, and schedules of classes from adult schools. Discuss, and write details on the board. Help students investigate interesting courses.

EXPANSION

- Have a career counselor talk about educational and career opportunities. With the class prepare questions in advance.

REVIEW

IN THE TEXT

Partner Interview

- Follow the suggested procedures on page T4.

Write

OBJECTIVE: To transfer oral information to written form.

- Read the instructions with your class.
- Circulate; help as needed.

Tell the Class

OBJECTIVE: To process information and address a large group.

- Students may either read their journal entry or tell the class the information from it, whichever format they are more comfortable with. Encourage other students to ask questions.

Cross-Cultural Exchange

OBJECTIVE: To compare music and special native dances in different countries.

- If all of the students in the class are from the same culture and you are from a different culture, have them teach you a dance and introduce you to some music.
- If everyone, including you, is from the same culture, see if any students can perform a special dance or piece of music for the class. Perhaps they can teach others the dance. Or invite another class to attend their performance.

EXPANSION

- Review all the transparencies or picture dictionary pages in this unit as individual **VOCABULARY CHALLENGES**. Give the class five minutes to write down all the vocabulary they can remember from an illustration. (No looking in the book or at notes!) Then have them report back informally, and make a master list on the board. Have them copy from the board any words that they didn't remember.

UNIT TEST

- A **conversation test** and a **vocabulary test** for this unit are located in the back of this Teacher's Guide, plus suggestions for administration. Feel free to make as many copies as you need.

TESTS

To the Teacher

ORAL CONVERSATION TEST

Conversation Test Evaluation Form

- This evaluation form is designed to be a quick, easy way for instructors to give feedback on students' conversation performance. It includes four major skill areas, with subsections of each. To complete the form, check off a grade of A, B, or C for each skill area and also check each subsection that may need work. If a student's conversation skill is below a grade of C, leave the boxes under the grades blank and simply check every skill that needs work under **Needs Work**. The only fill-in section is the subsection labeled "Other" in Vocabulary. Since vocabulary is so varied, an instructor may want to name a specific vocabulary topic here, such as "colors," "weather," or "hardware store".

- If your program includes more than one teacher at each level or more than one level, share the evaluation form with colleagues before using it in class. Decide together what will constitute A, B, and C grades at each level.

- As part of the class review before a test, distribute copies of this evaluation form to all students. Review the form together. Explain and demonstrate what will be needed for an A, B, or C in each unit, and remind students of the meaning of each of the sub-categories under **Needs Work**.

- During the Conversation Tests, you will be evaluating two students concurrently. To avoid confusion, fill in the top section of both students' evaluation forms before beginning your evaluation.

- Listen for these four things from each student:

  1. **listening comprehension:** How well does the student understand his or her partner? (If the partner's pronunciation is unintelligible, don't deduct from the listener. In such a situation, repeat a question yourself. Encourage the students to say, *I'm sorry. I didn't understand. Could you repeat that, please?*)

  2. **clear speech:** Is the student's speech intelligible? (If you have focused on any specific pronunciation points in this unit, remind students that you will be listening for those in particular.)

  3. **non-verbal communication**: Are the students' eye contact, gestures, and distances from their partners appropriate? Do the students express confidence?

  4. **vocabulary:** Can the student use the vocabulary practiced in this section, particularly in situations related to the student's own personal experiences? Does the student know the polite expressions associated with this unit?

Review Before the Test

OPTION 1
- Use the Review page at the end of each unit for each review.

OPTION 2
- Either pair students or divide the class into groups.
- Instruct the pairs or the groups to use their texts as a reference, and write ten questions from the unit to ask their partners or their group.
- Ask the pairs or the groups to share some of their questions with the class. Write some of them on the board but don't ask for answers.
- Once you have several questions on the board, practice asking and answering together as a class. Then have the groups or pairs ask and answer the questions they wrote.
- For further review, ask some of the questions again. Call on individual students for answers.

Conversation Test Procedure

- Either fill in the evaluations yourself or have one or more colleagues from outside the class assist in the evaluations; this will shorten the time the testing takes. (**Variation**: In some class situations, you may want to have the students evaluate each other. Care must be taken so that students being evaluated don't feel embarrassed and/or threatened.)
- Have students pair up in the most efficient way, without any confusion. For example, have students sitting adjacent to each other be partners, if that works in your classroom.
- Review the questions together. Be clear on your expectations. For example, tell the students the time limits for their preparation, if you expect them to respond with full statements, etc.
- Distribute the tests. Have partners prepare as quietly as possible. As they are preparing, help as needed. Especially during the first few "tests," students may need very specific guidance and support.
- Circulate; listen to the pairs interviewing each other. (First, Student A asks the questions and B responds; then students reverse.) Evaluate students on their questioning and answering skills. (Variation: Videotape some interviews and play them back; keep comments positive only!)

Alternative Conversation Test Procedure

If your class is large or time is short, you may want or need to test more quickly.
- Prepare a name card for each student.
- Shuffle the cards and form them into a deck of cards with names down.
- Pick a card, ask that student a conversation question, and record a grade or comment about his or her performance on the card. If the student needs another chance, ask a second question and grade the better answer.

WRITTEN VOCABULARY TEST

Review Before the Test

- Before administering this test, review the vocabulary and some of the activities in the text with your students.
- Direct the class to turn to a page in the **Activities** section of their notebooks.
- Show the transparencies for each lesson in the unit. If you do not have transparencies, use the illustrations in the text. Point to individual items and ask questions such as *What is this? What is he wearing? What is he doing?* Have students write the answers. (Variation: Have students respond orally at first, then write the answers.)
- To clarify this part of the test, explain that this is a written test of vocabulary recall and spelling for written communication. When learning English, developing literacy skills along with conversation skills is useful reinforcement for both skills. The test allows the students and you to evaluate their progress and determine what further studying needs to be done.

Written Test Procedure

- Before students begin the individual written test, remind them to work alone and not to talk during the test. Instruct them to raise their hand and ask you any questions they have. (That way, the whole class will benefit from the question and the answer.)
- Either correct the written test in class together, or grade the tests and return them to the students as quickly as possible. Either review the test together as a class, or meet with students separately (especially those who might have done poorly on the test).
- Keep tests in individual student portfolios with their work. Remember that everyday responses in class are far more indicative of students' true progress and achievement than a testing situation. Each time students take a unit test, have them check their progress in listening comprehension, vocabulary, pronunciation, and spelling by reviewing previous tests in their portfolio. This will help them learn self-evaluation skills.

EVALUATION FORM for CONVERSATION TEST

Student's name:_____

Evaluator's name: _____

Unit:_____

Date: _____

	A	B	C	Needs Work
1. Listening Comprehension	☐	☐	☐	___ Listening ___ Asking to repeat
2. Clear Speech	☐	☐	☐	___ Pronunciation ___ Intonation ___ Grammar
3. Non-verbal Communication	☐	☐	☐	___ Eye Contact ___ Gestures ___ Distance ___ Confidence
4. Vocabulary	☐	☐	☐	___ Polite expressions ___ Other: _____

UNIT 1: WELCOME TO CLASS CONVERSATION TEST

Partner Interview

Instructions

1. *Practice asking and answering these questions with your teacher.*
2. *Practice the questions and answers with your partner.*
3. *Write two more questions with your partner.*
   Practice these questions and answers together.
4. *Do your best when your teacher is listening!*
   First Partner A asks and Partner B answers.
   Then Partner B asks and Partner A answers.

Questions

1. What is your name?
2. Where are you from?
3. What language do you speak?
4. What do you wear to school?
5. What colors do you wear?
6. _____ ?
7. _____ ?

UNIT 1: WELCOME TO CLASS VOCABULARY TEST

I. Draw a picture of yourself. Write about your picture.

_____

_____

_____

_____

_____

_____

II. Look at the family picture. Answer the questions.

1. How many people are in the family?

   _____

2. How many women and girls are in the family?

   _____

3. How many men and boys are in the family?

   _____

4. How many people wear glasses?

   _____

5. What pets are in the family?

   _____

III. Answer the questions.

1. What are you wearing today? (include clothing and colors)

   _____

2. Is your family big or small?

   _____

3. How many brothers and sisters do you have?

   _____

4. What color are your eyes?

   _____

5. Are you married?

   _____

UNIT 2: EVERYDAY LIFE CONVERSATION TEST

Partner Interview

Instructions

1. Practice asking and answering these questions with your teacher.
2. Practice the questions and answers with your partner.
3. Write three more questions with your partner.
   Practice these questions and answers together.
4. Do your best when your teacher is listening!
   First Partner A asks and Partner B answers.
   Then Partner B asks and Partner A answers.

Questions

1. What is your name?
2. How are you today?
3. What time do you get up in the morning?
4. How many hours do you sleep at night?
5. What is your morning routine?
6. What do you do during a break?
7. What do you do every day?
8. _____ ?
9. _____ ?
10. _____ ?

UNIT 2: EVERYDAY LIFE VOCABULARY TEST

I. What is the man doing? Write about his morning routine.

1. _____

2. _____

3. _____

4. _____

5. _____

6. _____

II. What things are in your classroom?

1. _____
2. _____
3. _____
4. _____
5. _____
6. _____

III. Answer the questions.

1. What time do you eat lunch?

    _____

2. Who do you eat lunch with? What do you talk about?

    _____

3. Do you come to class on time every day?

    _____

4. Does your English class have a break?
   What different things do the students do during the break?

    _____

5. What do you do in your English class?

    _____

UNIT 3: THE CALENDAR CONVERSATION TEST

Partner Interview

Instructions

1. *Practice asking and answering these questions with your teacher.*
2. *Practice the questions and answers with your partner.*
3. *Write three more questions with your partner.*
   Practice these questions and answers together.
4. *Do your best when your teacher is listening!*
   First Partner A asks and Partner B answers.
   Then Partner B asks and Partner A answers.

Questions

1. What is your name?
2. What is today's date?
3. What is the weather today?
4. What do you like to do on a rainy day?
5. What do you want to do today?
6. Tell me about your favorite season.
7. What is your favorite holiday?
8. _____?
9. _____?
10. _____?

UNIT 3: THE CALENDAR VOCABULARY TEST

I. What are these people doing? Write about them.

II. Write the days and months.

Days of the week

1. _____
2. _____
3. _____
4. _____
5. _____
6. _____
7. _____

Months of the year

1. _____
2. _____
3. _____
4. _____
5. _____
6. _____
7. _____
8. _____
9. _____
10. _____
11. _____
12. _____

III. Answer these questions.

1. What day is today? What are you going to do today?

   _____

2. What day is tomorrow? What are you going to do tomorrow?

   _____

3. What day was yesterday? What did you do yesterday?

   _____

4. What was last month? Were there any holidays? Which ones?

   _____

5. When is your birthday? What did you do on your birthday last year?

   _____

UNIT 4: FOOD CONVERSATION TEST

Partner Interview

Instructions

1. Practice asking and answering these questions with your teacher.
2. Practice the questions and answers with your partner.
3. Do your best when your teacher is listening!
   First Partner A asks and Partner B answers.
   Then Partner B asks and Partner A answers.

Questions

1. What do you have for breakfast every day?
2. What do you usually have for lunch?
3. What are your favorite fruits and vegetables?
4. What kinds of junk food do you like?
5. Tell me about your favorite food.
6. What food don't you like?

Partner Role Play

With your partner, write a role play. Present it to the class.

Location: restaurant
Roles: customer, waiter or waitress
Action: order a meal

UNIT 4: FOOD
VOCABULARY TEST

I. **Write about this picture.**

_____

_____

_____

_____

_____

_____

_____

II. What fruits and vegetables do you remember?

Fruits	Vegetables
1. _____	1. _____
2. _____	2. _____
3. _____	3. _____
4. _____	4. _____
5. _____	5. _____

III. Answer the questions.

1. What are your favorite fruits?

_____

2. What vegetables don't you like?

_____

3. What vegetables do you like in a salad?

_____

4. Is it a good idea to eat red meat? Why or why not?

_____

5. What is your favorite dessert?

_____

6. How often do you skip breakfast?

_____

7. Where do you eat lunch?

_____

8. What is your favorite sandwich?

_____

9. How do you prepare it?

_____

10. What supermarket do you like to shop in? Why?

_____

UNIT 5: HOMES CONVERSATION TEST

Partner Interview

Instructions

1. Practice asking and answering these questions with your teacher.
2. Practice the questions and answers with your partner.
3. Do your best when your teacher is listening!
   First Partner A asks and Partner B answers.
   Then Partner B asks and Partner A answers.

Questions

1. What is your address?
2. Where do you study at home?
3. Tell me about your favorite room.
4. Tell me about your neighbors.
5. Do you ever have problems at home?
6. Tell me about one of them.

Problem Posing/Problem Solving

1. With your partner, choose a problem at home.
2. Decide what to do about it.
3. Present the problem and the solution to the class.
   (Partner A presents the problem; Partner B presents the solution.)

UNIT 5: HOMES VOCABULARY TEST

I. Write about the problems you see here.

1. _____
   _____
   _____
   _____

2. _____
   _____
   _____
   _____

3. _____
   _____
   _____
   _____

4. _____
   _____
   _____
   _____

II. What things are in your home?

Kitchen

1. _____
2. _____
3. _____
4. _____
5. _____

Living Room

1. _____
2. _____
3. _____
4. _____
5. _____

Bathroom

1. _____
2. _____
3. _____
4. _____
5. _____

Bedroom

1. _____
2. _____
3. _____
4. _____
5. _____

III. Answer the questions.

1. What is your address?

   _____

2. Where is the best place in the world to live?

   _____

3. How often do you sing in the shower?

   _____

4. What do you do in the kitchen?

   _____

5. Where do you watch TV?

   _____

UNIT 6: SHOPPING CONVERSATION TEST

Partner Interview

Instructions

1. *Practice asking and answering these questions with your teacher.*
2. *Practice the questions and answers with your partner.*
3. *Do your best when your teacher is listening!*
   First Partner A asks and Partner B answers.
   Then Partner B asks and Partner A answers.

Questions

1. How often do you go shopping?
2. Tell me about your favorite store.
3. Where do you usually go shopping?
4. What do you buy?
5. Which stores don't you like?
6. Why don't you like them?
7. Do you ever shop with credit cards?
8. Which cards do you use?
9. Which store in your neighborhood has the best prices?
10. Tell me about the store.

Partner Role Play

With your partner, write a role play. Present it to the class.

Location: *any store you choose*

Roles: *customer, sales person*

Action: *make a purchase*

UNIT 6: SHOPPING VOCABULARY TEST

I. What can you buy in these stores?

Toy store

1. _____
2. _____
3. _____

Office supply store

1. _____
2. _____
3. _____

Electronics store

1. _____
2. _____
3. _____

Hardware store

1. _____
2. _____
3. _____

Pharmacy

1. _____
2. _____
3. _____

Jewelry store

1. _____
2. _____
3. _____

Shoe store

1. _____
2. _____
3. _____

Sporting goods store

1. _____
2. _____
3. _____

II. Write a list.

You have $1,000 to spend in a department store. Make a shopping list.

Item	Price
_____	_____
_____	_____
_____	_____
_____	_____
	Total: _____

III. Answer the questions.

1. When do you go shopping? _____
2. What is your favorite flower? _____
3. Where do you usually buy your clothes? _____
4. What do you buy in a discount store? _____
5. What do you like to shop for at a mall? _____

UNIT 7: COMMUNITY CONVERSATION TEST

Partner Interview

Instructions

1. *Practice asking and answering these questions with your teacher.*
2. *Practice the questions and answers with your partner.*
3. *Do your best when your teacher is listening!*
   First Partner A asks and Partner B answers.
   Then Partner B asks and Partner A answers.

Questions

1. Tell me about your neighborhood.
2. How do you come to class?
3. What transportation do you use to go shopping?
4. Do you use a bank? What do you do there?
5. Do you ever go to the post office? What do you do there?
6. Is your community safe?
7. Are people friendly in your community?
8. Tell me about your community.

Partner Role Play

With your partner, choose a picture from this unit. Write a role play about the picture. Present it to the class.

Describe

Look at the picture on page 112. Tell your partner what is happening.

UNIT 7: COMMUNITY VOCABULARY TEST

I. Write about this neighborhood.

_____

_____

_____

_____

_____

II. What can you do in these places?

Post Office

1. _____
2. _____

Bank

1. _____
2. _____

Laundromat

1. _____
2. _____

Gas Station

1. _____
2. _____

III. Answer the questions.

1. When should you call the police?

   _____

2. When should you call the fire department?

   _____

3. Who do you call on the telephone?

   _____

4. What is your favorite kind of car?

   _____

5. What buildings are in your community?

   _____

UNIT 8: WORK CONVERSATION TEST

Partner Interview

Instructions

1. *Practice asking and answering these questions with your teacher.*
2. *Practice the questions and answers with your partner.*
3. *Write three more questions with your partner.*
   Practice these questions and answers together.
4. *Do your best when your teacher is listening!*
   First Partner A asks and Partner B answers.
   Then Partner B asks and Partner A answers.

Questions

1. Do you have a job? Tell me about it.
2. What job do you want in the future?
3. In your opinion, what job benefits are important?
4. Are there any reasons to keep a bad job? What are they?
5. What work do you like to do? Why?
6. What work don't you like? Why?
7. What do you want to do on your next vacation?
8. _____ ?
9. _____ ?
10. _____ ?

Partner Role Play

With your partner, write a role play. Present it to the class.

Location: on the job

Roles: boss, employee

Action: fire an employee for one of these reasons:
  • the employee is lazy
  • the employee is always late
  • other _____

UNIT 8: WORK
VOCABULARY TEST

I. **Who are these people? Write about their jobs.**

1. _____

_____

2. _____

_____

3. _____

_____

4. _____

_____

5. _____

_____

6. _____

_____

II. What do you remember?

Safety signs

1. _____

2. _____

Job benefits

1. _____

2. _____

Animals on a farm

1. _____

2. _____

Problems at work

1. _____

2. _____

III. Answer the questions.

1. What was your first job?

   _____

2. What hours do you work? _____

3. What is a good reason to quit a job? _____

4. What is a good reason to fire an employee?

   _____

5. What work do you do at home?

   _____

6. In your opinion, what is "men's work" at home? What is "women's work"?

   _____

UNIT 9: HEALTH CONVERSATION TEST

Partner Interview

Instructions

1. *Practice asking and answering these questions with your teacher.*
2. *Practice the questions and answers with your partner.*
3. *Do your best when your teacher is listening!*
   First Partner A asks and Partner B answers.
   Then Partner B asks and Partner A answers.

Questions

1. What do you do to stay healthy?
2. How do you treat a cold?
3. How do you treat a toothache?
4. Did you ever get hurt in an accident?
5. Tell me about it.
6. What hospital is nearest to your home?
7. How often do you go to the dentist?
8. Do you have a pet? What kind of pet do you have?
9. When do you take a pet to the veterinarian?

Partner Role Play

With your partner, write a role play. Present it to the class.

Location: *on the telephone with the receptionist for (choose one):*
  - *the doctor*
  - *the dentist*
  - *the veterinarian*

Roles: *receptionist, you*

Action: *make an appointment*

UNIT 9: HEALTH VOCABULARY TEST

I. These people are sick. What's wrong? Write about each one.

1. _____

_____

2. _____

_____

3. _____

_____

4. _____

_____

5. _____

_____

6. _____

_____

II. What do you remember?

Medical emergencies	Reasons to see a dentist
1. _____	1. _____
2. _____	2. _____

Reasons to see a doctor	Ways to stay healthy
1. _____	1. _____
2. _____	2. _____

III. Fill in the blanks.

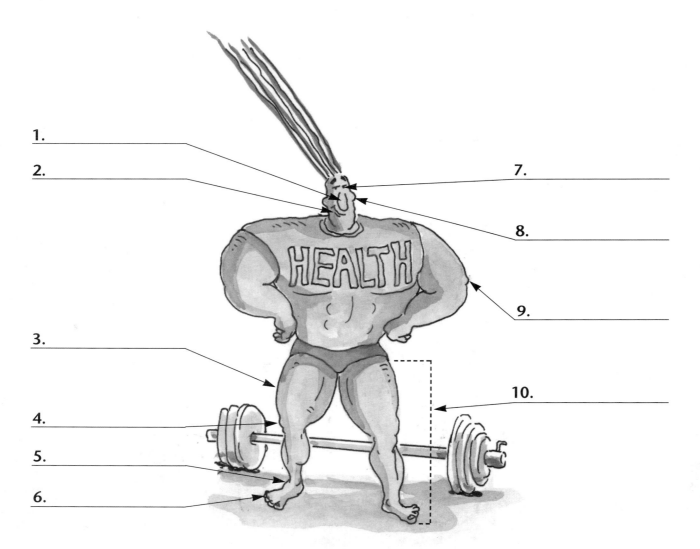

1. _____
2. _____
3. _____
4. _____
5. _____
6. _____
7. _____
8. _____
9. _____
10. _____

UNIT 10: LEISURE CONVERSATION TEST

Partner Interview

Instructions

1. Practice asking and answering these questions with your teacher.
2. Practice the questions and answers with your partner.
3. Write two more questions with your partner.
   Practice these questions and answers together.
4. Do your best when your teacher is listening!
   First Partner A asks and Partner B answers.
   Then Partner B asks and Partner A answers.

Questions

1. What do you like to do in your leisure time?
2. What is your favorite sport?
3. Tell me about it.
4. What kinds of movies do you like?
5. What is your favorite movie?
6. What do you like to watch on TV?
7. Tell me about your favorite trip.
8. What is your favorite kind of music? Tell me about it.
9. _____?
10. _____?

Describe

Choose a picture from Unit 10. Tell your partner about the picture.

UNIT 10: LEISURE
VOCABULARY TEST

I. What are these people doing? Write about each picture.

1. _____

_____

2. _____

_____

3. _____

_____

4. _____

_____

5. _____

_____

6. _____

_____

II. What are some leisure activities?

Individual sports

1. _____

2. _____

Team sports

1. _____

2. _____

TV programs

1. _____

2. _____

Types of movies

1. _____

2. _____

III. Answer the questions.

1. What wild animals are in the zoo?
   _____

2. What is the last movie you saw? Where did you see it? Did you enjoy it?
   _____

3. What is your favorite leisure activity?
   _____

4. What is your favorite place for vacation? When you go there, what do you pack? _____
   _____

5. Where is the closest library? What do you do in the library?
   _____

6. What is the next course you would like to study? Why do you want to take the course? _____
   _____

A WRITING BOOK Correlations

Units	AWB	ACB 1A	ACB 1B	ACB 1
1. HANDWRITING	1			
Print with Uppercase Letters	2–4	3, 5, 33, 65	7, 36, 47, 65, 71, 78	3, 5, 33, 65, 97, 126, 137, 155, 161, 168
Print with Lowercase Letters	5-7	8, 17, 21, 26, 51, 53, 60, 67, 71	42-43	8, 17, 21, 26, 51, 53, 60, 67, 71, 132-133
Print with Upper and Lowercase Letters	8-9	2, 3, 7, 24, 31, 33, 40, 49, 55, 59, 65, 79, 80	xxviii, xxix, 7, 14, 9, 21, 23, 53, 55, 63, 67, 87, 89, 95, 100	2, 3, 7, 24, 31, 33, 40, 49, 55, 59, 65, 79, 80, 97, 104, 109, 111, 113, 143, 145, 153, 157, 177, 179, 185, 190
Write with Uppercase Letters	10-11	3, 5	xxviii, 7	3, 5, 97
Write with Lowercase Letters	12-14	8, 17, 21, 26, 51, 53, 60, 67, 71	42-43	8, 17, 21, 26, 51, 53, 60, 67, 71, 132-133
Write Your Signature	15	3, 31, 65	xxviii, 55, 67, 95	3, 31, 65, 145, 157, 185
Write Time Abbreviations	16	18-23, 67		18-23, 67
Write Dates	17	28-29, 32-33	55, 95	28-29, 32-33, 145, 185
2. JOURNALS	19			
Personal Information	20	2-7, 10-12, 65	xxviii-xxix	2-7, 10-12, 65
My Family	21	10-11		10-11
Today	22	16-21, 26-29		16-21, 26-29
In the Morning	23	17-23, 50		17-23, 50
Weather	24	36-38		36-38
My Favorite Holiday	25	28-29, 32-33		28-29, 32-33
Thinking about Life	26	24, 27, 75-76	80-100	24, 27, 75-76, 170-190
Beliefs and Opinions	27	76-77	14, 25, 38-39, 50-51, 56-57, 73	76-77, 104, 115, 128-129, 140-141, 146-147, 163
A Day at Work	28	20-21	42-53	20-21, 132-143
3. GREETINGS	29			
Birthday Cards	30	30-31	10	30-31, 100
Valentines	31	32		32
Mother's Day Cards	32	10-11, 32-33		10-11, 32-33
Congratulations!	33		4-5, 10	94-95, 100
Thinking of You	34	62-63, 76-80	4-5, 10, 26-27, 50-53, 64-70, 74-77, 94-95	62-63, 76-80, 94-95, 100, 116-117, 140-143, 154-160, 164-167, 184-185
Get Well Cards	35		10, 64-65, 68-71	100, 154-155, 158-161
Sympathy Cards	36		4-5, 10, 68-69	94-95, 100, 158-159
4. ADDRESSES AND POSTAL SERVICES	37			
Addresses	38	65		65
Abbreviations of Street Addresses	39	65		65
Ordinal Numbers	40-41	65		65
Abbreviations of States	42-43	65		65
Abbreviations of Titles	44	65		65
Addressing an Envelope	45-46		26-27	116-117
Envelopes with Special Instructions	47-48		26-27	116-117
Hold Mail	49		26-27, 94-95	116-117, 184-185
Change of Address	50-51	65	26-27	65, 116-117
Express Mail	52		26-27	116-117

Units	AWB	ACB 1A	ACB 1B	ACB 1
5. NOTES AND MESSAGES	53			
Daily Planner	54	20-21, 26-29		20-21, 26-29
Notes to Yourself	55	20-21, 26-27, 58-59, 78-79, 82-83	6-7, 18-19, 26-29, 38-40, 66-67, 83	20-21, 26-27, 58-59, 78-79, 82-83, 96-97, 108-109, 116-119, 128-130, 156-157, 173
Telephone Messages	56-57	78-79	4-5, 20-23, 64-69	78-79, 94-95, 110-113, 154-159
Absence and Late Notes	58	14-15		14-15
Early Dismissal Notes	59	14-15	99	14-15, 189
Permission Slips	60		83, 98	173, 188
Notes to the Teacher	61	14-15	99	14-15, 189
Making Signs	62-63	14-15, 56-59	6, 10, 16-18, 30, 33, 47, 71	14-15, 56-59, 96, 100, 106-108, 120, 123, 137, 161
Notes for a Bulletin Board	64-65	14-15		14-15
Cancellation and Postponement Notices	66	36-38	91, 99	36-38, 181, 189
6. INVITATIONS & THANK-YOU NOTES	67			
Birthday Party Invitations	68	30–31	10	30-31, 100
Invite a Friend	69		20-21, 82-83	110-111, 172-173
Letter of Acceptance	70		82-83	172-173
Letter of Regret	71		82-83	172-173
Wedding Invitation	72	10	10, 82-83	10, 100, 172-173
Response to Formal Invitations	73-74	10	10, 82-83	10, 100, 172-173
Invitation to an Honored Guest	75		10	100
Thank-you Note for a Gift	76	30-33	10	30-33, 100
Thank-you Note for a Visit	77		10, 94-95	100, 184-185
Thank-you Note for Help	78	76-77	10	76-77, 100
7. HOME AND HEALTH	79			
Salad Recipes	80	44-45		44-45
Soup Recipes	81	44-47, 58-59		44-47, 58-59
Dessert Recipes	82	48-49		48-49
Menu Planning	83-84	42-60	63	42-60, 153
Supermarket Shopping List	85	58-59		58-59
Saving Money with Coupons	86	58-59		58-59
Comparison Shopping	87	58-59		58-59
Rental Agreement	88-89	62-65, 78-79		62-65, 78-79
Housing Complaint	90-91	78-79		78-79
Shopping for Home Repair Supplies	92	78-79	2, 9, 39-40	78-79, 92, 99, 129-130
Pharmacy Shopping	93		6-7, 64-65, 68-69	96-97, 154-155, 158-159
Health Insurance Form	94		56-57, 66-70	146-147, 156-160

Units	AWB	ACB 1A	ACB 1B	ACB 1
8. TRAVEL	95			
Giving Directions	96	65	16-19, 31, 34, 36	65, 106-109, 121, 124, 126
Directions from School to Home	97	65	16-19	65, 106-109
Directions to the Library	98		18-19, 98	108-109, 188
Directions to the Park	99		18-19, 92-93	108-109, 182-183
Directions to the Hospital	100		18-19, 68-71	108-109, 158-161
Driver License Application	101-102		32-33	122-123
Geographical Regions	103	34-39, 62-63	94-97	34-39, 62-63, 184-187
Vacation Postcards	104	5, 62-63	94-97	5, 62-63, 184-187
Letters about a Visit	105-106	62-63	94-97	62-63, 184-187
Customs Declaration	107-108		94-95	184-185
9. MONEY, BANKING, AND CREDIT	109			
Writing Amounts of Money	110	49, 55, 59, 60, 91, 92	5, 7-11, 27-29	49, 55, 59, 60, 91, 92, 95, 97-101, 117-119
Writing Checks	111-112	91	28-29	91, 118-119
Recording Checks	113		28-29	118-119
Overdrawing an Account	114		28-29	118-119
Saving Money	115		28-29	118-119
Automated Teller Machines (ATM)	116		28-29	118-119
Withdrawing Money	117		28-29	118-119
Credit Card Application	118-119	91		91
Credit Card Finance Charge	120	91		91
10. EMPLOYMENT	121			
Cover Letter	122		42-43, 54-55	132-133, 144-145
Résumé	123-124		54-55	144-145
Employment Application	125-126		42-43, 54-55	132-133, 144-145
Social Security Card	127			
Employee Withholding Allowance Certificate (W-4)	128-129		56-57	146-147
Request for Earnings and Benefit Estimate Statement	130		57	147
U.S. Income Tax Return	131-132			
Unemployment Weekly Benefit Statement	133-134		52-53, 56-57	142-143, 146-147
11. BUSINESS WRITING	135			
Business Letter: Request for Information	136-137		18-19, 36	108-109, 126
College Information Request	138		98-99	188-189
Classified Ads	139		12-13	102-103
Car Ads	140		32-34	122-124
Mail Order	141	82-83, 90-92	2-3	82-83, 90-93
Returning Merchandise	142	82-92	2-14	82-104
Complaint about a Billing Error	143			
Free Offers	144			
Cancelling a Subscription	145			